Living together in a World falling apart

Living together in a World falling apart

Dave & Neta Jackson

Creation House
Carol Stream, Illinois

Published by Creation House,
499 Gundersen Drive, Carol Stream, Illinois 60187.
In Canada: Beacon Distributing Ltd.,
104 Consumers Drive, Whitby, Ontario L1N 5T3.

Graphic design by Walles/Masterson.

Printed in the United States of America
by Bethany Fellowship.
First printing, March 1974
Second printing, June 1974
Third printing, March 1975
Fourth printing, March 1976

International Standard Book Number 0-88419-055-2
Library of Congress Catalog Card Number 73-82857

I pray that they may all be one, O Father, that the world may believe that You sent Me.

Jesus Christ

Contents

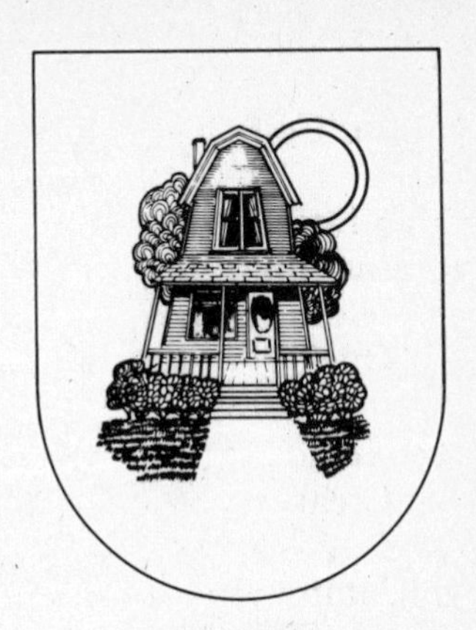

Preface

Family, friends, neighbors, people at work, churchgoers—each group a separate sphere, seldom overlapping. Share a little of yourself with many, but all of you with no one. It's a strange isolation in the middle of crowds, frustrating and fragmenting and pulling you apart . . . until, meeting no one who relates to your whole being, you wonder who you are.

Quick. Jobs change, people move, marriages collapse, and soon a familiar neighborhood and best friends are three houses and six years back. Old people live in the past, bewildered by a world they never prepared for. Younger ones strive for some tomorrow, never able to squeeze satisfaction out of the present. Propaganda presses from every side until your selection of truth is exhausting and unsupported. Crime in your streets, corruption in government. Whom can you trust? What can you do?

The family—what is it? What does it mean? A tiny unit boxed in isolation, shouldering every major and minor decision, joy and trouble that affects you by yourself? Even the family that hangs together (and that's an accomplishment these days) is soon flung apart, and you hold your grandkids once a year and spend your last days in a retirement home.

The Church—what is it? What does it mean? You grasp desperately for God's presence and find yourself in a half-empty pew. You seek new life, and find the congregation a pale shadow of the peace and meaning worded from the pulpit.

Where are the moorings, the stable points of orientation?

Whether it's called "future shock" by Alvin Toffler, the "last days" by Christians expecting Christ's return, or merely the passing of "the good old days when life was sane," the chaos we all sense is real and getting worse.

But we've heard enough from the prophets of doom who have no answers. This book is about church-community—the holistic environment God has always intended for His people. It provided joy and strength for the early Christians facing an equally hostile environment, and it works today in Christian communities all across the country. We've visited twelve of these communities in their various stages of growth; we live in one ourselves.

We've found that living in a church-community provides a channel for the power of the Holy

Spirit to minister to situations where "free-lance" Christians flounder and are mocked for their impotence. The church in community is a strategy for faithfulness and wholeness, from the first century through the "last days."

Part 1

Our First Attempts at Community

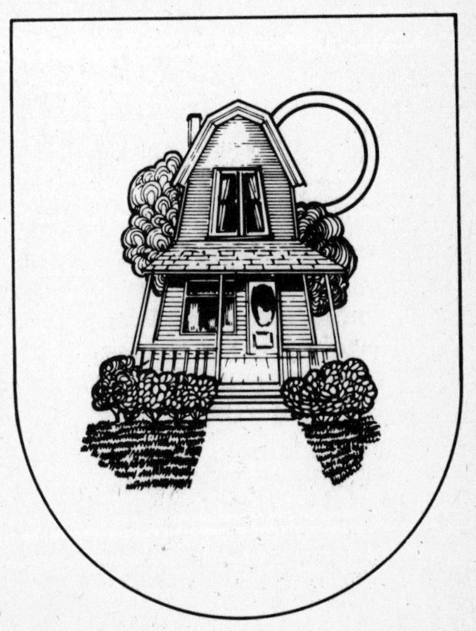

1

We Began

(DAVE)*

We began living in an extended family household more than four years ago. At first it was a naive, somewhat desperate effort to arrest our slip toward a treadmill we didn't want to be on. We were concerned about the emphasis on material things and the lack of community spirit so prevalent in our society. Yet the very life-style and value system of middle-class America in which we were involved seemed to make it hard to do much about these problems.

As an American family, we had been expected to be independent and self-sufficient. Materially,

---

*To tell this story more personally, Neta and I have written from our own unique perspectives. The writer is identified under each chapter title.

we did our best not to need anyone else. We'd been struggling through many of our problems alone, afraid to admit our weaknesses or to ask for help. We had to keep up an image of strength and self-sufficiency. We didn't involve our friends in our *real* concerns, and they didn't involve us.

We were particularly frustrated because we had been raised in strong Christian homes where the biblical message of caring for one another had been emphasized, where seeking and doing the Lord's will was always to take precedence over mere financial questions. The Lord was trusted to provide for His faithful.

But somehow the pressures of modern society were making it increasingly difficult for us to live by the values we had been taught. We thought our church should constitute a community of believers capable of withstanding these pressures, yet it seemed to go along with things as they were instead of encouraging an alternative. The "pillars" of the church seemed as severely trapped by material concerns and alienation as most non-Christians we knew.

It was the birth of our son Julian that finally led us to choose a new way of life. Neta had given up her job. We had always said that money wasn't important to us, but without our second income and with the increased expenses of parenthood, we suddenly faced some hard realities. Now we would soon have to move from our small one-bedroom apartment to something larger. How could we afford it?

I was working at an interesting job as an editor of a Christian publication. But with increasing family responsibilities, I started to feel the squeeze to be more careful about taking editorial risks as a matter of conscience, particularly if they might have financial repercussions.

Worst of all, Neta's post partum blues didn't go away. She was thrilled with our baby but discovered that big doses of loneliness and isolation came along with the joys of motherhood. She missed the stimulation of the people at her office, the new ideas, the events, and the creative challenge of writing. When I'd come home at night she'd milk me for the details of the day so that she could have at least some vicarious involvement with the outside world. I got tired of doing instant replays.

One other thing was getting to us—the fear of irrelevance. As evangelicals with an awakening social consciousness, we wanted to live out our faith. We had joined a black storefront church to serve and learn and hopefully heal some of the wounds of racism. We wrote, we talked, we even marched to help end the war. We became ecologically conscious and did our thing to reduce waste and consumption. But all to what end? Could we really change anything?

Our release came in the form of some old Anabaptist ideas that changed hearts must result in changed lives, and that the primary purpose of changed lives is to be an example, the "city on the hill," to the world's system of how God's Kingdom does things. The individual, isolated Christian can do little more than harangue the world about its ills. But the Christian community should provide a working exhibit of God's way.

We put all these things together: our struggles with materialism and isolation, our increasing needs as a family, our realization of how futile our individual efforts were to "change the world." And we decided to choose an alternative that seemed more consistent with biblical principles. We suddenly realized we didn't have to wait for society or the system or the government or someone else to change. We could begin right where we lived, on a day-to-day basis.

Living together with other Christian families seemed a way to start. At first we hardly knew what we were doing and very little of why, but in spite of the skeptical grand silences of some friends and relatives, we felt the Lord was leading. It seemed a way to share, to dilute the selfish emphasis on personal possessions, to care about the lives of other people.

We looked for as many as four or five couples to start with. Plenty of young Christians were willing to talk about the idea, but only Jan and Gary Havens were willing to try it.

So that's how we began that fall in 1969—just our two families in a big farmhouse north of Wheaton, Illinois.

2

Then There Were Others

(DAVE)

At the time, we didn't know of any other Christian families who had chosen the common life in an *extended household,* to use the proper term. We didn't have the experiences of others to learn from—just a sense of our own needs and the broad biblical principles on how Christians should relate to each other.

The most immediate joy for Neta, and Jan, too, was companionship during the day. Gary and I had our respective jobs, so on the surface nothing changed dramatically in our schedules. But for the women, it was like another planet. They shared the household chores and cooking, took turns babysitting so the other could have free time, helped each other keep perspective on the minor tragedies of a baby's first year, spent time each day just talking and sharing as two adults.

It had an immediate effect on our marriage relationship. Instead of coming home to a frustrated, tearful wife, I usually found Neta relaxed and happy. Instead of having to pick up the pieces of her day, we could create and share an evening together.

Not long after we moved together, Gary and I were standing on the back porch steps, making plans for a vegetable garden the next spring, when suddenly Gary said, "You know, Dave, there's a real security in joining our lives together. I mean, if that old furnace in the basement blows up, it's not just *my* problem, it's *our* problem. That just takes a big load off my mind."

He was right. I felt it too: the freedom of knowing that we were in this thing together.

We began to learn what it takes to open ourselves, to get beyond the shell where we live so much of our lives. For one thing, we realized that even though we lived together in the same house, it was all too easy to lead separate lives. We decided to set aside one evening a week to talk with each other, share ideas, make decisions about our life together, and, eventually, to share feelings and air grievances.

There was something about two young families living together that made it easier, from our end, to open our home more frequently to other people; and other people found it easier to drop in on us. When Neta and I had lived by ourselves, we had frequently invited students from a nearby college to come over. But they rarely came. After our move together with Jan and Gary, kids began dropping in evenings or weekends and bringing their friends. One student said, "Before, I always thought I might be intruding on your privacy if I just dropped in. But since you're open enough to live with another couple—well, if you're busy, I can find someone else to talk to. I don't feel awkward."

We had planned at the end of a year together to evaluate our experience and decide whether to continue. As the months progressed and our experience seemed positive and joyful, all of us were sure we would continue.

Then I lost my job.

It was the first time I'd ever been fired, and it shook me up. Rather than turning to our household for stability and guidance, I panicked and grabbed the first job offer that came along. Jan and Gary were stunned. The new job meant we had to move away, so they had to find a new place to live as well, since the rent on the old house was too much for them alone.

And with that, our experiment evaporated.

But our hunger for community grew. After our move, we met and finally joined the people who came to make up an extended household called Common Circle in Lake Forest, Illinois. There were two couples—Dave and Becky Toht and ourselves, plus three singles: Dave Moberg, Dale Cooper, and Sharon Farmer.

By this time we knew we weren't alone in longing for a new way of life. We had made contact with Reba Place Fellowship, which in turn introduced us to other Christian communities in the Chicago area. Then in February, 1972, Reba Place was host to a weekend conference to which over twenty Christian communities from many states sent representatives. A few were as small and new as our own; others had had more experience. Besides Reba Place, which began seventeen years ago, several had the experience of thirty, even fifty years of life together. The size of some numbered well into the hundreds. Even a few Hutterite brethren were there, bringing their four-hundred-year history with them.

Our first reaction was amazement at how the Holy Spirit had been working in many different places and in many different people, bringing them out of all sorts of religious and nonreligious backgrounds—Catholic, Baptist, Brethren, Episcopal, charismatic, fundamentalist, Christian Science, agnostic. He was bringing them to Christ and together to live a life of mutual sharing in obedience to Christ. Many of these groups had been unaware of each other, yet showed mutual concerns.

These people not only worshiped together, but also shared their lives and homes, finances and decisions; they were responsible to each other for their jobs, relationships, family life, and responses to the world around them. We began to see a commitment to Jesus Christ which was more radical and far-reaching than anything we had imagined. We discovered that for many communities, a common life was not just an experimental alternative but a necessity, an essential departure from the secular way of life that has crept into our churches and homes and muffled our witness.

This book started that weekend. Common Circle wasn't alone; the Holy Spirit was moving in many places, reviving the Church's original form to withstand the pressures of these days.

After one of the sessions of that conference Neta and I went for a walk. For a long time we said nothing, kind of like after a movie that hits you so hard you can't respond. Finally I said, "Hardly anybody knows that's happening. How can we share it with our families, our friends, the strangers who come to Common Circle peppering us with questions? So many of our Christian friends are losing interest in the church because the organization they know is irrelevant to their needs."

Yet before we could write we needed to learn and experience much more. For more basic than our desire to tell others what was happening was our need to discover for ourselves and our own extended household the fullness of what it meant to be a church-community. We set out in July 1972 to spend three months seeing how others were living the common life. We decided to skip the secular ventures as well as the Jesus People houses and concentrate on permanent groups of Christians responsible to and for each other. By October we had learned a lot.

Part 2

Research on the Road

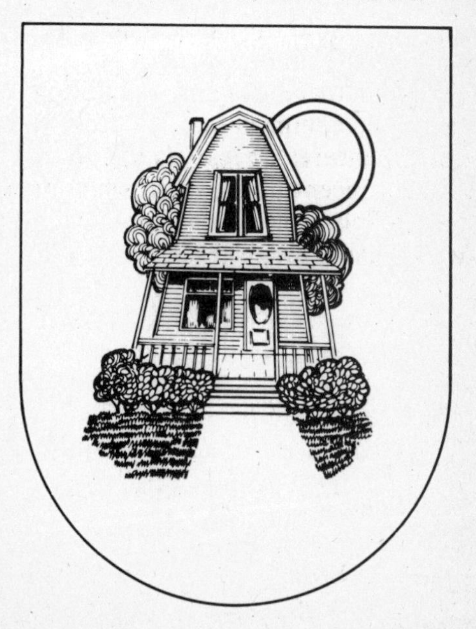

3

Five Communities

(NETA)

We visited a dozen communities in seven states that summer. A glimpse of life in five of them will provide a context for the subjects we will explore in the rest of this book.

Koinonia Partners

Before we ever set foot on the red earth of Sumter County, Georgia, we were well acquainted with the story of Koinonia from Dallas Lee's book, *The Cotton Patch Evidence.* Back, in 1942, Clarence and Florence Jordan with another couple put ground under a vision they shared for Christian community in the form of a run-down 400-acre farm near Americus, Georgia. Their purpose was twofold: first, to live together in community and to witness especially to the Christian teachings on peace, sharing, and brotherhood; second, to introduce scientific methods to local farmers. Others joined them, and in the early years the community lived at peace with its neighbors and made noteworthy contributions to the agricultural scene, particularly in poultry raising.

But eventually they became the object of mounting hostility because of their position against race prejudice. Their witness was not aggressively directed at others; they merely welcomed black people at their table and were happy to worship with them as well. So for years Koinonia withstood shootings, beatings, bombings, burnings, and an economic boycott. The violence finally subsided, but frustration set in. In the mid-sixties, Koinonia felt it was at the end of an era.

In 1968, Clarence Jordan and a few others met to discuss a new direction. Out of that meeting grew a burst of new life at the farm; they called the new arrangement "Koinonia Partners." New arrivals gave flesh to what Koinonians called "a new spirit of partnership with God and with our fellow man." They had three aims: (1) to communicate the radical ideas of the gospel at Koinonia and across the land through books, records, tapes, and speakers; (2) to instruct people in the ideas of Jesus at Discipleship Schools held at Koinonia and elsewhere; (3) to apply these ideas at Koinonia as a sort of demonstration plot of the Kingdom of God in farming, industry, and housing.

During our visit, we were put up in an extra trailer at Sunny Acres, a small cluster of buildings about a quarter-mile up the road from Koinonia's main complex. We were awakened our first morning there by the rumble of machinery as Bo Johnson, one of the farming partners, headed out into the fields. After a quiet breakfast by ourselves, Dave went to a meeting being held by a visiting monk.

Julian and I wandered around the farm trying to find someone who wasn't busy so we could talk. No luck. We finally drove our Volkswagen to Koinonia Village, a low-cost housing area built by Koinonia partners and volunteers for poor and displaced rural families, mostly black. Two dirt streets jutted off the main road, each lined by rows of cement block houses. The village was set into several acres of pine trees, and Julian's attention was immediately captured by a large playground.

Several Koinonia families also lived in the village; we found Jim Gauss at home, looking after his four children while his wife attended the meeting with the monk. Jim was reserved but friendly; he did share the fact that many people at Koinonia were worn out with the hundreds of visitors who keep turning up. A numbness was beginning to set in.

When the noon gong sounded through the woods, Julian and I returned to the main farm. Monday through Friday, a common meal brought everyone together from the various industries, the office, and the fields into the community dining room. But this was Saturday, so along with some other visitors we joined a group of singles for a hot lunch in their living quarters over the dining room.

Afterwards a guide took us down the road to a

second Koinonia Village then under construction. Sixty houses were planned for the next two years. We then had a chance to see the results of the various farming partnerships—vegetables, grapes, corn, peanuts, earthworms, and cattle.

Back at the main farm, our tour guide took us through the pecan-shelling, candy, and fruit-cake industry buildings. They were empty and quiet, the machines lying idle during the summer because of the heat. The other buildings were bustling with activity—the offices, the sewing industry, Koinonia Handcrafts. Many of the buildings were new, plain, one-story metal buildings, although a few, like the handcrafts workshop, had been made over from cow and harness sheds. Each of the industries had been designed to provide rural-based employment for poor people, mostly black, who were no longer able to make a living sharecropping Georgia farms. It was an effort to help stem the forced exodus of rural poor to the big city ghettos.

Over the next four days we met many of the twenty-eight adults who made up the core of Koinonia. Besides these "partners" and their families, about forty volunteers had come to work and explore community life on a short-term basis. They had been especially helpful in building the low-cost housing villages.

The families at Koinonia had separate living quarters (small cottages, duplexes, or trailers) while single members and volunteers were grouped together in cottages, rooms over the dining room, or up the road at Sunny Acres.

Koinonia paid no executive salaries. Each person or family in the community received a basic living allowance; anything beyond operating expenses for the farm went into the Fund for Humanity to help carry out the overall ministry of Koinonia Partners.

Unlike many of the other communities we visited, Koinonia Partners defined itself primarily through its outreaches and saw community—their life together—as a supportive life-style to make those ministries possible.

507 Atlanta Avenue

About a three-hour drive north of Koinonia is Atlanta. At the conference sponsored by Reba Place Fellowship we had become acquainted with two Christian communitites there—the Atlanta Fellowship and the one we chose to visit, simply called "507 Atlanta Avenue."

507 stands on the corner of Atlanta and Park Avenues across from Grant Park Zoo. As we climbed out of the car we were impressed with the size and graciousness of the rambling, two-story house and wondered how they managed to get such an ideal place for a communal household. Then we remembered what we'd been told: this was a racially changing neighborhood, and one of the purposes for this group of seventeen (seven singles, two couples, six children) that formed in September 1971 was to give time, witness, and effort toward stabilizing the neighborhood.

Another guest, a young mother named Patty, met us at the door and led us around, introducing us to the few people who were at home in midafternoon. Jean Shorthouse was out watering the vegetable garden in the backyard and keeping an eye on her own four children and several black neighborhood kids as well. Her two middle children were obviously adopted: Kristen, 4½, was Korean; Matthew, 2, beamed at us from under a loose, silky Afro. Our Julian joined happily into the hose-and-water play while we sat on the back steps and got acquainted.

There was no supper as such that night—Wednesday was the day they fasted in order to save food money (about $10 a week) to send to Bangladesh. So nearly everybody gathered around the huge handmade table for fried rice and water. Bill Milliken, a Young Life staff member in Atlanta and father of two, did the cooking.

Those staying home that night babysat for the lively Shorthouse and Milliken children. Their parents and several others in the group went to a planning meeting for an alternative school for children in surrounding neighborhoods.

We slept that night quite comfortably on day couches and a trundle bed in the basement playroom. 507 was sometimes flooded with visitors and had to put them in the singles' living room (out-of-bounds for the children) or on the sitting room couches or even on the floor.

507 had been much influenced by Koinonia Partners, seeing community as a means for Christians to reach out and touch the world in the name of the Kingdom of God. They had no formal commitment, but felt they were held together "by a common spirit of love for God and love for our neighbor." They did not identify themselves as a church and they did not have a common purse, though they often shared spontaneously. The household seemed to function in an orderly, if lively, manner, with everyone, men and women

alike, taking their turns cooking, doing dishes, housecleaning.

Church of the Redeemer

Unlike many of the communities we visited, Church of the Redeemer in Houston, Texas, *looked* like a church. This large Episcopal sanctuary on the corner of Telegraph and Eastwood Avenues spread out into an office and classroom-gymnasium complex which covered an entire block. However, around four hundred members of Church of the Redeemer lived "in community"—centering their lives in the church and its ministries.

Take the Hansen household, for instance, where we stayed. The compact, two-story house was a four-block walk from the church. We couldn't distinguish it from its neighbors until we met the people inside. Besides "Father Bob" Hansen (assistant rector at Redeemer), his wife Mary Carol, and their two children, ages ten and thirteen, there was: Paul, a young pastor-in-training who worked with Bob; Sherry, an occupational therapist; Brian, who spent each day at the church playing his guitar for various meetings or doing needed carpentry work; Jan, a young single who quit her job because she felt she was needed to help Mary Carol keep the household running smoothly; Mike, a long-term visitor who was once pronounced an "incurable schizophrenic" but had experienced healing within a loving, supportive, and well-disciplined Christian home; and Howard, a man in his fifties who, when he could find work, was an automatic transmission specialist—and totally blind.

These comprised only one of about fifty Redeemer households of various sizes with various purposes. Some were just a nuclear family plus one other person who needed shelter, encouragement, or a Christian family life. Others ministered to specific problems such as homeless children, drug abusers and alcoholics, or troubled marriages. Some households gave strength to a particular phase of the church's ministry, such as the one on North Main where staff members of the Way In coffeehouse lived and worked together. In some households certain persons were designated to work for money, supporting the rest who worked full-time for the church or ministered to persons in the home. A good wage earner who brought in more than his household needed might be moved to one needing more financial support; a person with a touch for children might be asked to join a household where that gift was needed.

This high degree of mutual sharing of gifts and resources within the Body had not always been true at Church of the Redeemer. Ten years before, the church had been dying. Many members had left, and those remaining experienced a humiliating failure to make the church relevant. The church's rector, the Rev. Graham Pulkingham, was disheartened to realize that his ministry was without power to do the things that the gospel of Jesus Christ promised. His heart hunger led him to realize, in his words, "that baptism in the Holy Spirit is a gift which Jesus had received from the Father and poured forth upon all flesh in fulfillment of promise—a blessing available to a *faithful* and *believing* church—

God's enabling gift for His church to be Christ in the world today."

Slowly, shepherded by the rector who now realized the power of the Spirit, the church experienced charismatic renewal. Daily teaching and sharing in the Scriptures replaced the dying programs, guilds, and organizations. Men, women, families began finding their way to Church of the Redeemer, seeking fellowship. A small, dedicated prayer band began to grow as member after member brought before them persons with indescribably difficult problems. They began to invite troubled ones to live in their homes, to experience the discipline, support, and stability of love. From personal experience the prayer band learned that God's Word and prayer, set in the daily fellowship of Christ's love, could heal every ill.

In response to the growing awareness that the Church is actually a daily fellowship, and that daily worship, teaching, sharing, and ministering should be possible, dozens of families began moving into the area within a five-block radius of the church. As they took troubled persons into their homes to minister to them, then added strong members to support that ministry, the congregation "slipped into community living, almost without knowing it," Father Pulkingham said.

Beyond the "ministering households," many other ministries and projects had come into being at Church of the Redeemer: the coffeehouse for young people; a shop where clothes were washed, ironed, and made ready for the needy; a ranch for boys with home problems or in trouble with drugs; a jail ministry; a counseling program; a free medical clinic; an office for free legal advice; a bookstore; a literacy program, especially to teach Mexican-Americans to read English; and a traveling ministry to other churches.

Church of the Redeemer's outreach, as one member put it, "grew out of our life together. The Lord spent about four years building us up and strengthening us as a Body before flooding us with those who come today in need of love, ministering, healing." Each member we talked to felt himself responsible to the Lord for his own life of faith, but also realized that the Christian life was meant to be a corporate life; that the Lord used individuals, but He used them best when they were bound together in faithful and loving harmony.

Society of Brothers

New Meadow Run, just outside Farmington, Pennsylvania, is one of three American communities of the Society of Brothers. It has around two hundred forty persons. (Woodcrest, in Rifton, New York, has about three hundred, and Evergreen, in Norfolk, Connecticut, about two hundred fifty. A fourth is located in England.)

The sign for New Meadow Run along Highway 40 was topped by a rustic plow, the symbol for the society's Plough Publishing House, which does its printing at New Meadow Run. Behind the sign we could see a large, green meadow sweeping up to what was once a resort hotel. We turned onto a shaded drive that meandered around the meadow, across a quaint bridge near the swimming pond, and to a secluded parking area. Along the way we were struck by the many flower plots, intricately landscaped springs, and paths by the lane, and the wooden play equipment set up on the meadow. Girls ran across the grass in bright, flowing skirts and peasant blouses; their long, bouncing braids were wreathed in garlands of flowers. The chalet-type buildings around the meadow and nestled against the wooded hills reminded us of a peaceful, European village.

We were graciously welcomed and brought lemonade and cookies in a small, knotty-pine lounge in the main building. Then we were shown to our room in one of the communal houses—gayly decorated with fresh flowers, a tiny dish of candies, balloons tied to Julian's crib, a welcoming sign with our names on the door. Down the hall from us lived a spry grandmotherly lady, and further on, a family with several children. Each family had its own set of rooms, but in the specially designed and recently constructed houses, two families shared a small kitchenette and a set of washrooms, bath, and shower.

New Meadow Run, like the other *Bruderhofs* (as their communities are called), gladly welcomed visitors, provided we were willing to share in their life and work. The next morning Dave went with most of the other men to work in the toy factory, which produced the sturdy wooden toys called "Community Playthings" often seen in kindergartens, nurseries, etc. This was the community's main source of support. After leaving Julian in the children's house, where he easily slipped into the three-year-old group, I shared work with a group of other women in the community kitchen, which prepared two common meals each day (breakfast was eaten with one's own family). On other days, Dave helped hoe corn along with several of the men and a group of young people; I was assigned to the community laundry, folding and sorting clothes.

The Society of Brothers is a good example of what might be called a total, but not closed, community. Each *Bruderhof* has its own school up through eighth grade, and adults not involved in the toy shop or in the publishing house contribute to the life support of the community—teaching, caring for children, gardening, or working in the community kitchen, laundry, office, etc.

The Society of Brothers was formed in Germany after the shambles of World War I as a Christian alternative to the wartime spirit which glorified loyalty to the fatherland above the dictates of God and conscience. Their purpose, in their own words, was "to live out the Sermon on the Mount." Their common life of sharing and responsibility for one another attracted many young people and families, who responded to their witness of practicing the principles of the Kingdom of God not merely in word but in deed. Their refusal to participate in war also attracted the attention of Hitler's Gestapo, which in 1937 ordered them to dissolve. Instead they fled, first to England, then on a dangerous journey by sea in the midst of war to Paraguay, where they settled for twenty years. In 1954, they emigrated to the United States, establishing their first community in New York State.

Community life is based on the society's expression of Christian brotherhood, where all property is held in common and all decisions and policies are based on unanimity in the Spirit. Children and family life were obviously chief joys, along with all forms of community work. Everyone, including older young people, spent part of the day in some form of community work, and as we worked beside them, we sensed a joy in "doing this for one another."

Joy was probably the most pronounced characteristic of the *Bruderhof*. Singing marked the mealtimes and could be heard often in the family homes; little dramas and folk dancing celebrated special events; the children's gay art work was everywhere.

Religious language seemed absent from their daily speech. Yet we knew from their books and history that service to God was the focus of the community. When we inquired about this, one of the members replied, "If you're not experiencing the presence of God in our lives, we have failed you." We were used to *talking about* Jesus and the Christian life a great deal more, but the brothers had not failed us; we did experience God's presence among them. Later another member said, "Words are cheap. Only when a person clearly sees His presence in the life we live can we effectively talk about what that means."

Dave later mentioned that their practice reminded him of certain Old Testament Hebrews who had such reverence for the name of God that they reserved its use for only the most sacred occasions.

Reba Place Fellowship

We visited half a dozen other communities that summer, and eventually wound up back in

Evanston, Illinois, to take a closer, longer look at Reba Place.

The fellowship had grown considerably over the last year or so, now numbering 140 adults and children. They owned twelve buildings, all within walking distance of each other. Several families lived in rented apartments nearby. Some of the members of the community had organized into six ministering households on the order of Church of the Redeemer in Houston. One occupied a four-flat apartment building while the others lived in large three-story houses.

We arrived on a Friday evening, just in time for the once-weekly common meal. The small children had been fed at home and were playing now while the adults and teen-agers gathered at long tables in the house at 727 Reba Place, which is also used for meetings and worship. After supper someone announced that the fellowship had purchased a storefront building to remodel for meeting space to meet Reba's recent rapid growth.

The impetus to launch this community came from Goshen College in Indiana, which in the forties was taking a new look at the radical Protestant reformation in the sixteenth century and the Anabaptist concepts which gave birth to such groups as the Hutterite and Mennonite communities. These communities of believers were, at that time, radical and creative alternatives to the church as institution. They constituted the revival of a line of brotherhoods said to have existed in an underground fashion since the time of Constantine, with roots in the first-century Church. Several of the Goshen graduates began taking these same concepts seriously as applicable to Christians in the twentieth century. Three of them bought the first house on the small street called Reba Place in 1957, and the group began to grow.

On Sunday we again gathered in the crowded meeting room for worship. Guitars, recorders, and an autoharp accompanied joyful folk-type songs of praise. Occasional clapping and arms lifted in praise added heart and soul to the music. Appearance varied; we could see long dresses and short, beards and smooth-shaven faces, suits and jeans.

A play from the life of Jeremiah captured young and old alike. And afterward the biblical message was more fully explained by one of the community leaders. Several children asked questions about the play and received careful answers.

Spontaneous sharing and praise formed the last part of the worship service. People prayed at once for each prayer request; a woman thanked God for His help that week and in response someone spontaneously started a song of praise. This went on for about forty-five minutes, until we were overwhelmed with the Spirit's presence and the work He was doing here.

Reba Place Fellowship felt called to be a church, a radical example of love and sharing in the midst of society. They committed themselves to each other, to seeking God's will for each other, and to doing Christ's work *as* the Body of Christ. To obey Christ they worked for peace and justice in the neighborhood and around the world. A black landlord who owned a large apartment building nearby told us, "I'd do most anything for the fellowship. Eight years ago this part of Evanston started to change racially. Whites got scared and started to leave. Things deteriorated rapidly. Then the fellowship did a little neighborhood organizing, and the downhill trend stopped. Now this is one of the most peacefully integrated neighborhoods in the Chicago area. And it's stable too."

The fellowship also operated a neighborhood day care center and recently had begun a common-work industry partly manned by guests there for healing or learning.

Most working members of the fellowship, however, held various jobs around the Chicago area as teachers, blue-collar workers, social workers, psychologists, even a computer programmer. They put all their income into a common purse, which even replaced insurance policies for medical and other emergency expenses. After distributing personal and family living allowances, they used the remainder "to further God's Kingdom," whether by (1) meeting the needs of a family within their own group who had no wage earner, (2) supporting a person within the group who had been designated to give time in a nonpaying ministry, (3) or by underwriting needs and ministries outside the community.

But most important, the fellowship saw its task to be bringing people into the Kingdom, introducing them to Jesus Christ as Savior and Lord, and inviting them into a tangible, visible Body where they could discover and use their gifts. They gave their lives sacrificially for others who came to Christ so they could provide a supportive environment which met their needs as learning, growing Christians.

4

Similarities

(DAVE)

The communities we visited were similar in certain crucial ways. Most important was the great emphasis placed on the teachings of Jesus as the life-directing principles Christians are to live by.

Where this perspective was evident we found no negation of the inspiration or importance of the rest of Scripture, but merely a different balance than was common to our background. I'd somehow received the impression over the years that the Epistles were the core of my faith and Christ's words, particularly in the Sermon on the Mount, were a poetic, somewhat impractical introduction.

However, we saw on our trip that where Christ's words were regarded as the core, the rest of Scripture took on the tone of a handbook of specifics, and Christians emphasized love, peace, forgiveness, sacrifice, joy, gentleness, goodness—the characteristics of God's new order. This message is in the Epistles, too, but it seems that when Christians de-emphasize Christ's words they bog down in doctrinal disputes.

In at least three communities the special attention to Christ's words and their implication led to the writing of valuable expositions and study guides on the Sermon on the Mount. Eberhard Arnold, the founder of the Society of Brothers, wrote *Salt and Light*. John Miller, one of the early members of Reba Place Fellowship, wrote *The Christian Way*. And Clarence Jordan, the founder of Koinonia Partners, wrote a book titled *The Sermon on the Mount* (see bibliography for details).

Another similarity growing from the emphasis on Jesus' teachings was the clear witness for peace and nonviolence in almost every community we visited. There seemed to be no debate about whether the life that Jesus talked about could include killing people. The quiet readiness among these believers to lay down their lives to be faithful to Christ's teaching greatly encouraged me.

I had spent five years in the military, during which time God had to really knock me over the head before I would affirm Christ's call for peace. After great turmoil I finally applied for and received a conscientious objector's discharge.

But in some of the communities we visited we met Christians who had personally faced violent threats and attacks from Hitler's Gestapo and the Ku Klux Klan without yielding their antiwar, nonviolent stance.

And a peculiar problem for a Christian community is that in times of persecution it is highly visible. It's the "city on the hill" that cannot hide. When that city announces that it is the expression of God's Kingdom rather than of the state or society, a stage is set which looks very much like that of the early Church.

Two other similarities seem also to have resulted from a commitment to Christ's teachings: the common life and the sharing of money and possessions. Not all communities had a common treasury, though that seemed the most frequent and practical way of equitable sharing. The goal seemed to be to provide for all rather than accumulate private fortunes.

A consciousness of the presence and power of the Holy Spirit was also evident in many of the communities. Not only was He the presence of God with them but the one by whom God revealed His will. Whether it was a decision-making meeting of the whole Body where God's revelation was waited for in quiet silence, or the confidence of an elder to do what was needed in a touchy situation, the communities trusted the Holy Spirit to guide.

And He did in a way that affirmed and strengthened their trust time after time, so that the community was able to proceed with boldness.

Jesus' way of love was also a crucial characteristic. When asked to identify the most important kind of law or guideline for a godly life, Jesus answered that the Law was summarized in two commandments to love: "You shall love the Lord your God . . . . You shall love your neighbor as yourself" (Matthew 22:37-39).

These commands were not separate but interrelated. Jesus made it clear that love for God became manifest in the love we show others.

Christ loved us with a sacrificial love, and He expects that our love should be the same kind. "We know love by this," John wrote, "that He laid down His life for us; and we ought to lay down our lives for the brethren" (I John 3:16). Christ died sacrificially on the Cross. We are admonished to "be a living sacrifice" and "take up our cross daily" and follow Him. Immediately following the apostle's admonition in I John 3:16 to "lay down our lives for the brethren," he gives a very practical example of what he means: "But whoever has the world's goods, and beholds his brother in need and closes his heart against him, how does the love of God abide in him? Little children, let us not love with word or with tongue, but in deed and truth."

We manifest love for Jesus through self-denying love for our brothers—daily, practical, cost-us-something love. Not only are we the Body of Christ by virtue of the unique and individual relationship with Him, but in our relationships with each other we suffer the same kind of sacrificial love that Christ's own body suffered for us.

There are times in these days when one would think that Jesus had said, "By this shall all men know that you are my disciples, by your buildings, by your worship services, by your clergymen." But He had little to say about these three most prominent characteristics of the Church in our time. He spoke instead about the way of love. "By this all men will know that you are My disciples, if you have love for one another" (John 13:35). This is what identifies God's people gathered together. This is what the world should witness. This is the greatest similarity we saw in the communities we visited: God's people in active, loving relationships.

Part 3

The Heart of Community: Relationships

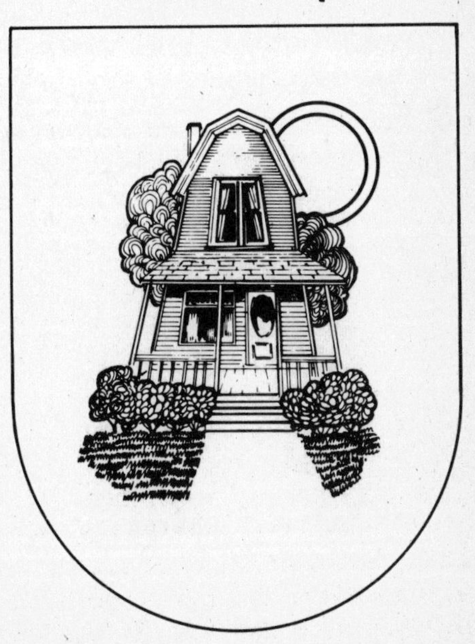

5

Free-Lance Christians

(DAVE)

Most of us live in a world so socially fragmented that unless we have been in a Christian community such as Reba Place, we may have difficulty picturing the relationships involved.

"We often feel a sense of community in our church," friends sometimes say. Unfortunately, that feeling is to real Christian community what an occasional maternal twinge is to being a mother. Mothers have constant relationships, not just periodic meetings or afternoon picnics. Likewise, a Christian community touches and integrates every area of a member's life. Members cease being "free-lance" Christians doing their thing here and there. They become accountable to a specific Body and do Christ's work as revealed to that Body by the Spirit.

It's important to point out that this is not the emergence of a new gospel of communitarianism. We are speaking of returning to the original dynamic relationship between Christians that characterized the early Church described in the first part of Acts. This has since been the mark of many Christian Bodies down through the centuries. Community is the expression of love that Christ said would identify His disciples.

However, it is possible to be an active, devoted, doctrinally correct group of Christians without being a Christian community. Christ taught that love for Him had to be expressed between believers. He said that at the Judgment many would be surprised when He responds, "To the extent that you did it to one of these brothers of Mine, even the least of them, you did it to Me." (Matthew 25:40).

Christ was trying to wean the disciples off His physical presence and onto the reality of His Body made up of them when He said, "I am with you a little while longer .... Where I am going, you cannot come .... A new commandment I give to you, that you love one another" (John 13:33,34).

When Peter heard that, he wasn't interested in being weaned off Christ's physical presence. He boasted of his love and loyalty for Christ: "Lord, why can I not follow You right now? I will lay down my life for You."

But later that night Christ was arrested, and before morning Peter denied Him three times. After His resurrection, Christ confronted Peter again on the same issue, asking three times, "Simon, son of John, do you love Me more than these?" Three times Peter tried to answer yes, finally saying, "Lord, You know all things; You know that I love You." But Jesus said to him, "Tend My sheep" (John 21:15-17).

In a way, Peter was right. He did love Christ, and Christ knew it. But what Peter hadn't learned was *how* Christ wished him to express that love. Peter hadn't learned the significance of the new commandment. The moment Christ left physically, Peter went back to his private agenda of fishing—serving himself. He hadn't been weaned so that he could continue expressing his love for Christ by expressing it to the brotherhood, Christ's Body.

The time was almost past when Peter could express his love for Christ by following Him all over the countryside, listening attentively to His teachings, and bragging about his loyalty. After Christ's ascension, Peter could validate his "I love You" in only one way—He would have to care for Christ's sheep.

Most of us admit that today's church on the corner doesn't demonstrate wholehearted commitment and involvement between its members. Even the most devout are usually free-lance Christians who basically consider *themselves* the final authority in determining God's will for themselves. Consequently, most follow a private, though sometimes sacrificial, agenda for their lives. And it's a rare church these days where enough free-lance Christians get going in the same direction in the unity of the Spirit to show evidence of His power.

The longer we thought about these things, and the more we experienced our shared life at Common Circle, the more we were convinced that the church-community was significant in these times.

6

Community Is Relationships

(NETA)

I first met the friendly, dark-haired woman when she invited us to share a snack in her family apartment at New Meadow Run. Then I found myself working next to her the following afternoon in the laundry folding room. I was surprised to learn she was a brand-new grandmother; she looked much younger, her long hair caught back from her face by a thin silver band. She wore the conventional dress of the Society of Brothers —calf-length cotton gathered skirt, simple cotton blouse, shoes with white anklets.

But she wasn't a transplant from "the old country; in fact, she was from New York State. I was especially interested in someone who chose to leave behind typical American society for the total community of the Society of Brothers. "Why? What made you come?"

She told the story briefly, working steadily on the baskets of fresh-smelling clothes. "My husband and I were missionaries to Africa," she said. "Some problems developed, and without much warning, we were recalled to the States by the mission board. We were heartsick that our fellow missionaries had not had the honesty or openness to talk to us about any failures they saw in our work. We were disillusioned that the board would recall us before anyone dealt with us as persons."

The family settled back into life in New York once again and became involved in a local church. "But we were still faced with only superficial relationships," she said.

During this time a fire broke out in the dining hall of Woodcrest, the *Bruderhof* in Rifton, New York. Men from local churches in the area, including her husband, helped rebuild the structure.

"While working with the people at Woodcrest," she said, "my husband was struck by the deep relationships he observed, the sense of openness and honesty in relating to one another. When the rebuilding was completed, he brought the rest of the family to Woodcrest for an extended visit, then for many short stays. Finally we made the decision to join our lives together with the Society of Brothers.

"We hadn't been looking for a common life, for the total life together, but for deep and honest relationships," she concluded simply. "And we've found them here. It's a joy to live our lives openly in a loving way before our brothers. Our children are delighted here too. Our oldest daughter went away to school, married, then came back with her family to live."

This woman had touched on the simplest, yet most significant definition of Christian community: *Christians in loving relationship with each other.* We had somehow come to accept the lack of love in our relationships with church people until our decision to live with Gary and Jan made us face the question: how *should* Christians relate to each other?

The answer sounded obvious and simple: Christians should love each other. But the more specific questions were harder: Am I open with my brother? Am I honest about my feelings? Am I listening to his burdens, no matter how small? Can I accept a rebuke from him? Do I defend myself? Can I go to my brother if I feel he is doing something wrong? What do I do when I'm irritated by some petty action or remark? How do I handle my resentments against a brother? Am I willing to put aside my own desires and to serve him? What does "bearing each other's burdens" mean?

Reba Place Fellowship introduced us to a word that has been particularly helpful: *openness.* A pamphlet, "The Way of Love," published by the fellowship says, "Jesus once characterized the devil as a liar and the father of lies. The essence of the demonic, these words imply, is to distort reality. When this demonic activity penetrates into human relationships, it closes men off from one another. This is the darkness that poets and prophets speak of when they write of the devil and his works. The alternative to this is 'openness,' the honest giving of our lives to God and to one another in truth. This is the 'light' in which apostles and saints constantly encourage us to walk."

A verse we had known since childhood took on fuller meaning. "If we walk in the light as He Himself is in the light, we have fellowship with one another . . ." (I John 1:7). Light, truthfulness, nothing hidden. This is essential in our relationship with God and also with our brothers and sisters in Christ. Anything less destroys fellowship.

We began to experience the need for openness in the daily realities of living together at Common Circle. Someone used up Julian's baby shampoo without asking. I thought I knew who did it, but somehow couldn't bring myself to confront him; I let my judgmental attitude eat away inside and affect my relationship with this person. Or . . . I had a quarrel with Becky, but was too proud to confess that I was wrong, so I put on a nonchalant mask and hoped the whole thing would blow over. (It did, but only on the surface.) Unconscious hurts . . . hidden resentments . . . unspoken feelings . . . lack of forgiveness and being forgiven—little things that built walls between us and the brothers and sisters closest to us.

After being challenged by Reba Place and other communities on the spirit of openness, we began to do some Bible study about how Christians should relate to one another. In a discourse on being stumbling blocks to each other and breaking down fellowship, Jesus said, "If your brother sins against you"—irritates you, wrongs you, hurts you—"go and reprove him in private; if he listens to you, you have won your brother. But if he does not listen to you, take one or two more with you, so that by the mouth of two or three witnesses every fact may be confirmed. And if he refuses to listen to them, tell it to the church; and if he refuses to listen even to the church, let him be to you as a Gentile and a tax-gatherer" (Matthew 18:15-17). *Go to your brother.* Sounds simple, but it's one of the hardest actions on earth. All of us at Common Circle recognized that we'd rather take care of problems between us by ignoring them, hoping they'd go away. But feelings don't go away. They subside or are forgotten, but they crop up again, the next time a little stronger, a little harder to drive away. Feelings and resentments build a barrier between you and your brother —or a blow-up over an incidental matter.

At first we hesitatingly brought up our feelings in our group meetings. "That made me very irritated" or "I don't think you should have done that without asking" or "You acted as if I weren't important." It was less traumatic to begin in the group; somehow we felt less vulnerable and alone to have the others supporting the process.

During our visit with the Philadelphia Fellowship, a small but growing community in that city, Art Gish commented on openness. "At first we brought everything up in the group. But it became almost an encounter group, and that's not what we're about. We realized we were bringing things up in the group that we should have worked out brother-to-brother. In a way it was a great waste of the group's time and energy."

Someone at Reba Place Fellowship said, "We should come to our group meetings prepared to do God's business. It's up to each individual to ask himself if anything stands between himself and a brother or sister that would undermine the unified spirit we need for seeking God's will and worshiping together."

We talked about this together at Common Circle and realized that we were using the group to air personal grievances that we should have taken care of privately. But we also realized that living as closely as we do in our extended household, many matters affect the whole group. These we agreed to bring up in the group. Also, many times after two people worked out a grievance, they then shared it with us all. We found these occasions to be a witness to us, to cause rejoicing.

We barely began to understand the implications of Matthew 18 when we were struck by another passage. "Brethren, even if a man is caught in any trespass, you who are spiritual, restore such a one in a spirit of gentleness; looking to yourself, lest you too be tempted. Bear one another's burdens, and thus fulfil the law of Christ" (Galatians 6:1,2).

Both Jesus and Paul spoke about "if your brother sins . . . ." All too frequently my brother's sin becomes *my* sin because I develop a judgmental attitude toward him, or if the sin is against me, an unforgiving and hurt spirit. We have discovered about ourselves that one-sided sin rarely occurs. If my brother sins, almost every time I have to go to him and ask forgiveness for my attitude toward him.

"Restore such a one in a spirit of gentleness; looking to yourself, lest you too be tempted." Just going to my brother about a grievance is not enough. Going with an accusing spirit, a spirit of superiority, or "Ah ha! You've messed up again and I'm going to point it out to you" will only further tear down the relationship between us. I must go to him because I want to restore fellowship, humbly realizing that I'm not only capable of erring in the same way, but that I probably will and already have, and that one of the reasons I'm sensitive to his sin is because it's my problem as well.

So often we'd thought of these verses in the sense of "church discipline" connected with such specific and "big" sins as adultery or wife-beating or stealing from the church treasury. More to the point, these verses became part of our every day life when we realized that we sin against our brother whenever we "put him down," or build ourselves up at his expense, or irritate him by some thoughtless comment or action, or fail to recognize his needs.

It seemed strange to us that the command to bear one another's burdens came directly after this verse on restoring our brother. It was easy for us to think of someone else's burdens falling into the category of poverty or sickness. And these were burdens we needed to bear for one another. But in this passage, bearing one another's burdens seemed particularly to mean shouldering each other's weaknesses, failings, and sins. We were to come to our brother who had sinned because we were to bear his sin with him, take on his weakness and failings as if they were our own. We came to restore him. "I am with you in this. I am here to join you in going through whatever is needed in order to overcome this sin (or failing or weakness). I will stand beside you with all my strength and resources."

This morning I had an "out" with Sharon. We had no bread, and shopping day was tomorrow. She said we could do without—it was better than running to the store every day for piddling things. This irritated me. Often I've felt that Sharon's crusades for efficiency and resourcefulness in running our household stepped right over the needs of other people. I felt it especially this time, since Sharon doesn't eat much bread and the rest of us do. I confronted her and tried to explain why I felt irritated and thought it was all right to go get bread. She accepted it, but later I didn't feel a loving spirit between us.

Again I went to her and this time apologized. "I didn't mean to create hard feelings."

"I *don't* have hard feelings," she said impatiently, "but I surely wish you'd drop the subject. Too much has been made of it already."

Ouch. I know I have a problem of building up resentments, so this morning I'd been trying to get my feelings out right away. But sometimes when I'm honest about them, I make a big deal of something small. I went up to my room feeling I'd failed once again, and ended up crying and praying. A few minutes later Sharon knocked on the door, came in, and put her arm around me. Her touch was one of both asking to be forgiven and forgiving me; it restored our fellowship.

As we talked, I began sharing some other areas where I had feelings of failure. Sharon was able to encourage me and help me regain some perspective, even giving me some suggestions on what I could do. I hugged her and said, "Well, together maybe we'll learn the things the Lord is trying to teach us!"

And I felt that strongly. It's impossible to "bear one another's burdens" in this way apart from a close community of believers. My brother can't bear my weaknesses if he's not involved in my life, because he won't even know what they are. I can't go to him about some sin in his life if I'm not willing to do whatever it takes to help him overcome it and "bear with him" until fellowship is restored—with God, or with me, or with another brother.

In the Sermon on the Mount, Jesus gave us another thought to consider in relating to our brother. "You have heard that the ancients were told, 'You shall not commit murder;' . . . But I say to you that every one who is angry with his brother . . . shall be guilty enough to go into the hell of fire. If therefore you are presenting your offering at the altar, and there remember that your brother has something against you, leave your offering there before the altar, and go your way, first be reconciled to your brother, and then come and present your offering" (Matthew 5:21-24).

As we have come together in community, wanting to honor Christ and obey Him, we have had to face up to a hard fact: If we can't love the person(s) we live with, it's meaningless to send money to Bangladesh, or sing songs of praise, or read the Bible daily, or write a book on community, or witness to a stranger, or become a conscientious objector. Jesus meant that if there's something between us and our brother, then our gift or sacrifice to Him is meaningless. Jesus wasn't putting down the gift or the sacrifice. Rather He was saying that broken fellowship between brothers in Christ makes true worship and full obedience impossible. We're to take care of that first, Jesus said.

This doesn't mean that Christians should put other areas of obedience and worship aside until some mystical day in the future when we've "got it all together" as brothers in Christ. We'll need a lifetime to build relationships of love with each other. But it's putting the cart before the horse if a group spends all its time praising God or seeking ways to obey Him concerning the needs of the world if they haven't spent time learning to love each other.

Love each other! Why is it so hard? A friend of ours in a newly forming community remarked, "I'm ready to lay down my life for you, but I don't know if I'm ready to run upstairs and get your sweater for you." Sacrificial love isn't as interesting or dramatic on the everyday level. In fact, it's a good deal harder because it demands constant selflessness.

But as a Bible teacher pointed out to us at Church of the Redeemer in Houston, "If we're not afraid to die, then we are not afraid to lay down our lives *daily* for our brother. We're not afraid to initiate love."

Part 4

The Need for Specific Commitment

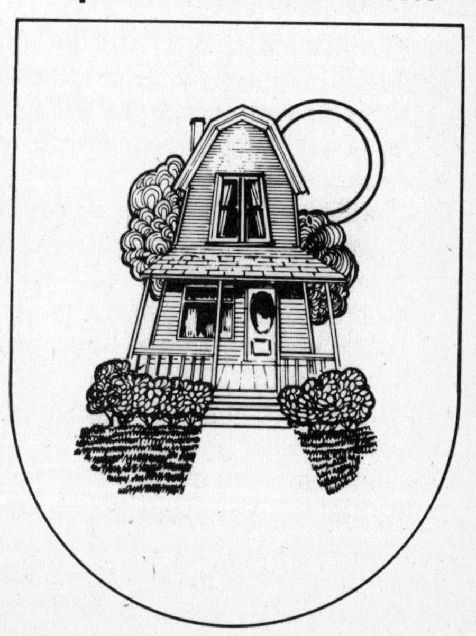

7
The Spirit of Commitment

(DAVE)

A visitor to a community is often struck first by the outward forms—the extended household, economic sharing, maybe a common work. But people can hardly share a common life unless they share a common motivating force. For the Christian community, it is essential to have a common commitment to the lordship of Jesus Christ. Out of this commitment grows the spirit of the community—a spirit of seeking and doing the will of God, a spirit of sharing with and serving each other as brothers and sisters in Christ, and a spirit of living in the Kingdom of God now.

The lordship of Jesus Christ

Most important in a Christian community is the person Jesus Christ, the Son of God. To make anything else, even the concept of community, the central focus would be idolatry. For a church-community, neither structure nor brotherhood nor radical causes can provide the rallying point or motivating force. Jesus is the one we are to lift up, worship, and follow.

This was the spirit we found in the communities with genuine life. Each person was there for one purpose: to seek and do Christ's will. It was in the environment of a life together that the Holy Spirit provided the direction and power to make that possible.

Everything else was subservient to a commitment to Christ's lordship. For instance, the structure of community became important only because it provided a vehicle for obedience, and it was through obedience that we recognized Christ's deity and lordship. A Hutterite brother once told us, "The Bible nowhere commands that Christians live in community, but it is almost impossible to apply the commands of Christ without it."

We can see how central Christ is from the way He said we should express love for Him: "To the extent that you did it to one of these brothers of Mine, even the least of them, you did it to Me" (Matthew 25:40). This was not a pantheistic suggestion that God was really nothing more than corporate humanity; Jesus is God, whom we worship in spirit now that He has returned to the Father. But we also worship Him when we obey His command to love our brothers and sisters.

Christ is the reason and focus for a joyful life of community.

The spirit of sharing and serving

If the purpose of our life is to do the will of our King, a number of attitudes result. One is a spirit of sharing and serving, a spirit that characterizes the commitment of people gathered in a church-community.

We were impressed with the pervasiveness of this spirit at the Society of Brothers. The morning after we arrived, I went over to the woodshop with many of the other men to help build the wooden toys they sell.

I worked with a young man at a machine that beveled the edges of small hardwood boards later used in toddlers' chairs. One after another I fed thousands of those boards into the machine. My newly found friend stood on the other side and took them out and stacked them. Later we traded and he fed while I stacked.

We talked above the noise. Physically the job was not hard. In fact, none of the jobs in the woodshop appeared particularly hard or demanded special skill. The shop was clean, well-organized, and had the finest equipment. "But how could I feel content doing this for the rest of my life?" I wondered.

I'd worked at factory jobs before, and usually they were my best motivation to do well in school! They were great for the summer or part-time if they paid well enough. I studied hard because I didn't want to turn a screw or feed a dryer in a plywood mill for the rest of my life no matter how much I'd be paid.

But here was a group of people who had chosen a group work that was neither intrinsically fulfilling nor personally rewarding in money or status.

Why then did they do it? And how could they talk about the joy of working?

Later in the day when I saw Neta, she had discovered the key for me. After breakfast she talked with one of the mothers as they washed the dishes. "Life here isn't lived according to what's in it for me," she had said, "but according to how I can serve others and thereby obey Christ." At the Society of Brothers there were no jobs that did not serve; therefore, if a person was able to find his reward in serving others, it made little difference what he did; there was meaning in it. In fact, even those at the *Bruderhof* who had jobs that we might call "personally fulfilling " learned not to derive meaning from ego inflation but from the service they offered others through it.

The next day I went back to the toy shop and tried on the new perspective. The work was different! I found joy in doing even the smallest task if it served others.

I imagined what it would be like to live there. What if they didn't need a writer right now, but someone to mow the lawns regularly? I began seeing how much my ego was tied up in my work and in everything I did that had status attached.

A long string of yeah-but's started going through my mind. *Yeah, but wouldn't that be a waste of my gifts? Yeah, but who would write for the Lord if I didn't?* And on they went. The Holy Spirit was there in that noisy toy shop. He kept reminding me of answers I already knew. For instance, the Spirit gives gifts as He pleases to build up the Body. If that local Body doesn't need someone to write, all my writing would fail to serve them or the Lord. But if the Lord did need a writer, the Holy Spirit would give the gift, and along with it He'd see that the local Body received the message and commissioned the right person to obey it. And above all, the Lord didn't need a writer who was writing for himself.

All around the Society of Brothers we saw the expressions of lives lived for others. A walk around the community was literally filled with joyful surprises—the abundant flowers and rock gardens planted by the young people as a "gift" to the others; carefully carved steps in a steep path; beside the lane a spring someone had landscaped with beautiful pools, waterfalls, moss, and flowers. In each family apartment we visited we saw paintings, trinkets and crafts that various community children had brought. Everyone stayed after lunch one day to help the vegetable-garden people snap beans. On another occasion, the young people painted a beautiful mural and sang specially practiced songs to welcome their parents and the other adults home from an outing. Each aspect of their lives seemed not a private gratification but a gift to others.

Christ said, "Whoever wishes to save his life shall lose it; but whoever loses his life for My sake shall find it" (Matthew 16:25). It was evident to me that the people at the Society of Brothers had found joy and meaning in laying down their lives for their brothers and sisters.

"We need to reemphasize the servant role of the church," a brother at another community declared to us a few weeks later. This spirit of serving—of laying down my self and taking up the cross in obedience to Christ—leads naturally to a spirit of sharing. If in obedience to Christ I am willing to give up all that I think I am, I need not hoard what I have. I can share it gladly.

One day a man dropped into one of the households at Reba Place Fellowship. He seemed troubled and wanted to talk. Virgil Vogt took him down to the little basement office where they could be alone. After a little bit of discussion, it appeared that the man had a severe drinking problem and was looking for "help."

Virgil told him, "Well, first I'll tell you about the best help we can give you." And he shared with the man the possibility for a new life in Christ. The man grew a little uncomfortable. "Well," he broke in, "what I really need is some money for a bus ticket to Cleveland." His voice was challenging, implying that Virgil was probably willing to hand him "religion" but wouldn't go so far as to actually give him money.

"O.K." Virgil agreed, "we can give that kind of help, too, if that's all you really want." He was quiet a moment, then he shook his head. "You know something?" he said, looking straight at the man. "You've just really let me off the hook. Because if you had chosen a new way of life in the Kingdom of God, then as your brother I would have had to lay down my whole life for you. This house, my time, all my money, whatever you needed to meet your needs would have been totally at your disposal for the rest of your life. But all you want is some money for a bus ticket . . . ."

The man was so startled he stood up and shortly left, without remembering to take the money. The next Sunday he was sitting next to Virgil in the worship service.

Living in the Kingdom now

Whether we were at Koinonia, influenced by Southern Baptist Clarence Jordan, or speaking to the Armstrongs at the Philadelphia Fellowship with their Catholic background, or with a family from Anglican background and now at the Society of Brothers, or with the Jewish-influenced Michael Friedmann at the Fellowship of Hope, we always saw an understanding about living by the standards of the Kingdom of God. It is the attitude expressed by Paul in Romans 13:12,13: "The night is almost gone, and the day is at hand. Let us therefore lay aside the deeds of darkness and put on the armor of light. Let us behave properly as in the day."

Christians do not belong to the old order (the night), but the new order (the day). We are governed by the ethical standards of the new order. Art Gish, from a Brethren background, put it this way: "We can't be sucked into the old liberal preoccupation of trying to make a sick world well. We're called to *act well* by the power of Christ. Nothing is more effective in darkness than to let the light shine. Talking about the light does no good, nor do efforts to wipe the darkness away."

This spirit affects life-style and ethics by allowing people to live in a noncompromising way. Means become as critical as ends. If we are living in the Kingdom rather than trying to get to it, or waiting for it, we view war and killing, for instance, in a different light. If such things have no place in the Kingdom of God, they have no place in our life now. This perspective provides a certain freedom from the charge of "unrealistic idealism."

It makes the ideal real and measures right conduct in terms other than success.

A spirit of living in the Kingdom now makes commitment possible because it doesn't weigh obeying Christ and sharing and serving in terms of whether they seem like wise plans at the moment. It asks only whether they are the characteristics of the Kingdom.

The Kingdom perspective causes the church-communities to see themselves as though they were colonies of settlers from another country, planted in a strange land, to bring to it the challenge of God's Kingdom and His way of being accepted in it—the gospel. They take seriously Peter's characterization of Christians as aliens and strangers here on earth.

Consequently, a network of Christian communities has developed across the country. Often when members travel, they stay with other communities. Sometimes they exchange food—some of the Hutterite colonies often send barrels of wheat and honey to other communities. Communities send money back and forth, too. The Shalom Fund paid our trip expenses; several groups set it up to help new communities and facilitate special projects. Sometimes members of one community make arrangements for a member to transfer to a school near another. Communities with problems sometimes request people with special pastoral or counseling gifts to come and help.

All this is reminiscent of the New Testament record of the early church-communities and, in fact, Christian communities whenever they have existed throughout the centuries.

Most Christians intellectually agree with the spirit of complete commitment. It may sound a little idealistic to them, but they usually admit that if taken all the way, "that's what the Bible calls for." However, when it comes to subscribing to some kind of structure that might help put that strong commitment into practice, they hesitate.

Sadly enough, the cause for such hesitation is frequently unbelief. It's more secure to keep your options open, not put all your eggs in one basket. Get the most out of this life and this world's system just in case.

8

Are We Exclusive?

(DAVE)

Like anyone, I had a problem with complete commitment. For a long time I wasn't really certain enough to go all the way. But I had another problem, too. I had adopted a mistaken liberal idea which said that any group which got too specific automatically became prejudiced.

In my senior year at Bible school in Portland, Oregon, I discovered that, consciously or unconsciously, the school had a history of keeping most blacks out of the day school, where they might fraternize with the student body. Willy, a freshman from Jamaica, was the only black to have attended for years. He, of course, would be going straight back to his island and knew better than to get romantically involved with white girls. American blacks found admission even harder.

The civil rights movement was just beginning to have its belated effect on me back then in '64. I was shocked as I became conscious of my own attitudes and actions; I was embarrassed because of the racism in the institutions I was involved in. Partially from guilt I went on a crusade to change school policies. At a student-faculty-administration retreat I, the editor of the student paper, challenged:

"Is this school open to blacks?"

"Why are there rumors that some have been rejected for 'academic reasons' when they had better grades than some whites who have been admitted?"

"Why don't the school's vigorous recruiting and ministry programs extend to churches in the local black community of ten thousand people?"

I guess I really believed that such a serious problem needed only to be pointed out to "good Christians" and they would make amends. But policies have hardly changed in the many years since, even though the school has doubled in size. The administrators and faculty responsible still deny any part in racism.

My embittered reaction was to determine to have nothing to do with any group that rejected anybody for any reason. Prejudice, I reasoned, was just too subtle. The only safeguard was to welcome without question anyone who walked in the door.

That overreaction gave me trouble later on; I didn't understand the important distinction between positive inclusion into something and a prejudicial exclusion.

This problem found its most unmanageable expression years later in an urban educational project I was involved in. The project tried to be so many things to so many people that it wasn't effective in a sustained way for anyone. We wanted to be open so that no one would feel excluded. We succeeded in being just about as open as a market square, but when people wandered in they didn't know what they were into. Neither did we. For at least the first eighteen months, the time I was on the board, we continually rehashed the goals of the project.

Anyone could attend the board meetings, and almost anyone could join. At least one person came to one board meeting, joined, said his piece that night, and never showed up again.

Everyone was afraid to put anything down in writing or get too specific about a commitment or membership requirements. After all, someone might charge us with being exclusive.

Occasionally we were praised for our openness, but usually we were condemned because we didn't know what we were about. In trying to include one person or group we ended up violating the interests of someone else. We wanted to be inclusive, but we had nothing certain to include anybody into.

Definition, I've discovered, at least gives everyone else the freedom of knowing whether or not he wants to be a part of that group. Then when a person is admitted, at least he's included into *something*.

One person on our trip put it this way: "There is no conflict about inclusiveness and exclusiveness. The more exclusive I am about my wife as my wife, the more freedom I have to relate to other women." As visitors and outsiders to many communities that summer, we found that where a group was clear on membership and commitment, they could relate to us freely. We didn't threaten them.

The more a group knows what it's about, the clearer the question of membership will become. Christ never presumed that everyone was in the Kingdom of Heaven. It was open to everyone, but a person had to face some requirements for entrance—basically the acceptance of Christ's kingship over every area of his life.

Christ's analogy of the Kingdom of Heaven to the wedding feast is appropriate. Everyone was finally invited, but only those who actually came got to take part. The people who refused to give up their other interests just weren't included. It would have been foolish to send out a little bottle of wine and a sack of goodies to those who were following their own agenda. Such pretense wouldn't have made a single one of them any more a participant in the party. In fact, it would have destroyed the intent and definition of the party.

The key to godly openness is to make everyone welcome and to require nothing of them that they cannot give—just themselves. But that, of course, is a big price.

If a person chooses the alternative, we cannot pretend otherwise. It is erroneous to think that in the name of freedom and openness all distinctions must vanish. The greatest freedom occurs when there are clear choices.

Today, when personal freedom is so frequently stressed, it is sometimes difficult to talk about a commitment that is going to bind someone to something. People are crying for a more meaningful, cohesive life at the same time they are demanding more "don't tie me down" freedom; they don't realize that often the two are incompatible. For a church-community to have any ongoing meaning, it must have form. That form will sometimes be personally restricting.

Alvin Toffler points this out in *Future Shock* when he says, "The very same writers who lament fragmentation also demand freedom—yet overlook the un-freedom of people bound together in totalistic relationships. For any relationship implies mutual demands and expectations. The more intimately involved a relationship, the greater the pressure the parties exert on one another to fulfill these expectations" (page 86).

In the church-community these expectations are affected by the standards of Scripture as well as the need for smooth interaction between people. The Bible is far more than a religious document. It is also a manual for life in the Kingdom, with instructions affecting every kind of human relationship, every personality trait, man's care of his environment, even the appropriateness of certain occupations. The whole analogy of dying to one's self and living anew in Christ presumes a certain loss of the freedom to do as we please.

But we can gain a new freedom that is far more valuable. It is the freedom from isolation amid the sea of people. It is the freedom to have our lives injected with meaning and purpose—with cosmic purpose. It is the freedom to have deep relationships with other people.

Christ described it like this: "The kingdom of heaven is like a merchant seeking fine pearls, and upon finding one pearl of great value, he went and sold all that he had, and bought it" (Matthew 13: 45,46).

9
Why Membership?

(DAVE)

From what we have observed and experienced, at least four main reasons show why a recognized membership is important. The first two primarily serve the nonmember. The second two are largely for the benefit of the community.

It is important to have a recognized membership in community so that an outsider or visitor is not scared off. He must have an acceptable way to relate to members wholeheartedly without shouldering full responsibilities. He must not avoid the open meetings for fear that any minute someone is going to ask if he's turned his paycheck in yet. He must be granted a place of free observation and learning until he is ready to submit himself. He must also know that his presence as an observer is not awkward or embarrassing to others.

As we traveled, we were often in the visitor position. We felt most comfortable as outsiders in communities where membership was clear. Sometimes we were invited to the usually closed decision-making meetings of communitites, but we didn't presume that we would be. When during those meetings delicate matters arose, we did not feel awkward. We knew that if the members were uncomfortable with our presence, they would have the presence of mind to ask us to leave.

On the other hand, we felt a little embarrassed a couple of times where membership wasn't clearly defined, because it would have been almost a personal affront for anyone to ask us to leave. Far from alienating us, membership put us as visitors at ease and made us feel welcome.

The church of Jesus Christ cannot be merely a clique of friends. It must be open to all who will follow Him, all whom He has called to walk the same road. Therefore, a recognized membership in a community serves the outsider in a second way. It assures him that this local expression of Christ's Kingdom is open to him when he chooses to align himself with it.

Recently we were visiting a community with no formally recognized membership. While we were there, a new family who were interested in the group expressed their insecurity. They said, "How would we become members? Just what would be expected of us? We'd like to keep worshiping with you. But we're not quite ready for some of the things you are talking about. Does that mean we aren't welcome? And when we're ready, how will we know if we've really been accepted?"

Any newcomer realizes that there are things going on in which he is not included, decisions made where he's not consulted. A very small community may get by with the old slide-on-in technique for incorporating new people, but when the church gets larger, that procedure promotes suspicion. People are tempted to wonder whether there is a "more inner circle" than they are aware of. Also, when the criteria for membership are not clear, the group is tempted to be a clique of friends where people are admitted or rejected on grounds that are too subjective.

In the same community where the newcomer family was trying to discover the path to fuller involvement (and whether they wanted to take that path), I recall another couple who thought of themselves as part of the group. But as one of the "members" said, "We knew they weren't completely committed, so we just took everything they said with a grain of salt."

It was true that the couple wasn't fully submitted—they abruptly moved out of the state against the counsel of the group. Regardless, nobody's comments and participation should be taken with a grain of salt unless they are fully aware of the reasons why and have chosen to remain in that slightly set-apart condition. Anything other than this is not only personally degrading, but results in closedness rather than openness.

The community thought they were being open by not setting up some kind of formal membership that would distinguish members from nonmembers, but the result was the opposite. The group had to continually judge the attitude of the couple. When membership is clear and determined by total commitment and submission, the outsider holds the key. Any time he wants to use it, he can come in all the way.

The first way that membership benefits the group itself is that the fully committed know what is expected of them. This avoids the rude shock of discovering that it is every area of a person's life that must come under the lordship of Christ. People are less apt to state, "No, no, I didn't sign up for that. You can have my money, but not my job"—or whatever.

The other area that membership benefits is decision-making. If a group believes it is the Body of Christ and that its purpose is to discover His will and do it, then it must be cautious about the sacredness of any time it comes together to conduct His business. That is no place for the nonbeliever to participate, because the Spirit does not reside in his heart. It is no place for the partially committed whose ear for God's will may be tuned more toward selfish interests. And it is no place for the partially informed (unless such a person is a visiting Christian and understands enough of what is going on to exercise mature judgment over his ignorance).

I have been in decision-making meetings where nonmembers of each of these three descriptions short-circuited the process of discovering God's will. God's business is too important to let that happen.

Historical records of early church-communities seem to indicate three types of meetings. One was a closed meeting for the committed members only, in which the group sought the Spirit's leading and strength. A second was a meeting especially designed for the instruction and teaching of potential or new members. The third was more evangelistic or worshipful, often conducted in a public place and open to all.

We've seen many communities (particularly the oldest and most stable) follow this pattern with great success.

So a recognized membership benefits both seeker and member. It need not be open to the charge of exclusiveness, but rather makes genuine acceptance possible.

10

A Community and Its Commitment: Philadelphia Fellowship

(DAVE)

We had escaped the South's summer heat by visiting the Tennessee and Georgia communities during an unseasonably cool spell. But when we turned north toward Philadelphia, we had to creep under the greenish brown edge of a thermal inversion. The air was hot, thick, and unfit. The radio warned older people or those with respiratory problems to remain inside.

We had met several people from this little community six months earlier at the gathering of Christian communities at Reba Place and were eager to see them again. But our spirits sagged as we fought the heat and the traffic for an hour and a half, getting lost in the jungle of an unfamiliar city. Finally we found the address where we were supposed to stay, a row-house in the Spanish section of town.

Dora Armstrong flung open the door and bubbled over with welcome in a slight Argentine accent. While Julian ran to their back steps to join their two girls in playing with the water hose, we sat down with Dora and her husband Tom to rest and talk. The cheer and gladness that surrounded us refreshed our sagging spirits—we felt at home with brothers and sisters.

The rest of the fellowship arrived at the Armstrongs awhile later with a potluck supper—a total of four families, one single man, and a handful of other visitors besides ourselves. The purpose of the evening was to give us as much time for discussion and questions as we wanted. The hubbub of the meal quieted into a short Bible study. Then as we shared in the darkening heat, we saw the steps they'd been taking as a community.

The group had begun about three years earlier as a peace group, but had developed into a fellowship to explore the implications of following Jesus Christ. They began talking community and were exploring their need to live closer together, maybe even develop some extended households—when they stopped short. They were moving ahead on the form of community without being clear exactly what their commitment amounted to.

So they plunged into hours of careful Bible study, discussion, and thought, and finally agreed on the essentials of the church-community they felt the Holy Spirit wanted them to be. During that time a few of the original group dropped out. But the nine who remained felt they had come to such singlemindedness that they could form a core the Lord could use. As one final step in their preparation, they "dissolved" the group about six months before our visit so that each individual person could be readmitted according to the commitment he had chosen to make.

This was something like the time of intense preparation of the disciples under Christ. It was necessary before they were ready to reach out as a unified body of believers.

The commitment they worked out was something they could write up, not to have a creed, but to have something specific to discuss when new people came who might want to join with the fellowship.

They gave us a copy and it reads as follows:

Group Commitment

I commit myself to this group, believing that we have been called by God to be a visible community of Christians seeking to follow God as we know Him through Jesus Christ. I have examined my life and believe there is nothing in my past and present relationships which would hold me back from full commitment to God and my brothers and sisters.

Together we affirm our commitment to:

God

We learn God's will for us through the Bible, prayer, counsel with other believers, and sensitivity to the Spirit.

We accept Jesus Christ as the resurrected Lord who is present, leading and teaching us.

We seek to obey God in all of life, whatever the consequences.

Each other

We commit ourselves to meet together regularly for worship, fellowship, working out our lives together, and for seeking corporate witness.

We will support each other, giving and receiving admonition in living a life of obedience to God.

We will help each one develop and use his abilities and achieve personal fulfillment.

We will come to decision by consensus, respecting each individual without coercion.

The world

We will care for God's creation.

We seek to be an example of Christian living.

We share with neighbors the good news, witnessing for peace and justice and confronting evil.

We seek to serve the needs of those around us and stand with the poor and the oppressed.

We are willing to go anywhere for the sake of the gospel.

It may seem a little unusual that after coming to agreement on a commitment, they would have to disband and reapply under the very terms they had agreed to recognize. But Jeff Wright explained it this way: "On something as basic as a commitment, it's not only essential for us all to come to a verbal agreement, but each of us must be confident that every other member interprets that commitment the same way. A little testing is appropriate, too, and I'm an example of the value of that.

"Near the end of the commitment you'll notice the statement that we intend to be a witness for peace and justice and to confront evil. Well, I had a part in inserting that line. I think those things are important—part of being Christlike. But I hadn't fully applied them to my life. At the time, I was working as a physicist for a munitions corporation developing a new, deadly laser weapon. The group confronted me on it by pointing out that my job seemed inconsistent with a commitment to be a witness for peace.

"Believe me, it was a rough struggle. The market is presently flooded with unemployed physicists, and I had no prospects of another job. What would I do if I quit?

"I was like the rich young man who came to Jesus. I agreed with what I needed to do, but it was so hard to do it. Finally, with the prayer of everyone else, I made that move of faith to follow Christ in the way I knew He wanted me to. Since then He's given me a new job consistent with the Kingdom."

After Jeff told his story, I could see the importance of what they had done. If they had failed to go through that painful process, they would have destroyed the value of their commitment. Definitions of what they meant would have soon blurred.

In a church I once belonged to, the pastor would question people asking for membership. Along with the basic questions about a relationship to Christ, he would ask, "In joining yourself to this church, are you willing to come when you are called and go where you are sent?" Those are powerful words and could have reflected a kind of commitment that would have meant a dynamic common life as the local, visible Body of Christ.

Except . . . they were meaningless. Everybody answered yes to that question, yet eighty percent of the members didn't even come to the regular Sunday services.

The initiation process of binding oneself to a commitment does not end the matter. A commitment is a declaration of intent to grow into the maturity of Christ Himself. It is never possible to take the basics for granted, but paradoxically the initial testing or questions of submission establish a foundation.

At Church of the Redeemer in Houston they spoke of commitment in terms of "being bound to the Cross of Christ by my brothers and sisters." When a person seriously declares his intentions to obey Christ, he establishes a foundation on which his brothers and sisters in community can help him build that life of obedience. When the temptation to do his own thing apart from God nearly gets the best of him, his brothers and sisters can remind him that he's decided to lay his own life down. Their help can bring consistency and strength to the real direction he wants his life to take.

But the process of maturity is never complete in this life (certainly not at the initial embrace of a commitment); therefore the wording of a commitment should be in terms of the infinitely perfect Christ to whom we are to be conformed.

While we were with the Philadelphia Fellowship, for instance, members were considering their attitude toward finances as an area of continuing maturity. One of those present was Art Gish, a man with a Church of the Brethren background whom we had first met through his books. "We feel that we aren't owners of any of the things that God has given us, but merely managers," he said. "That demands a spirit of sharing that we are trying to work out in actual daily life. I think that the minimum commitment for a community in the area of finances is financial accountability between the members. However, we are now considering a common purse. If we agree that everything belongs to God, and we are just allowed to use it in His service, why should some have more than others in our same fellowship? A common purse seems to be a practical way of sharing. But it isn't going to be easy, because it will mean some adjustment between differing life-styles."

After everyone left for the evening, we stayed up and continued to talk to Tom and Dora. It was still much too hot to sleep. Only occasionally did the air move a little through the two front-room windows. Outside, older Spanish-speaking kids still hung around the front stoops. In that area of the city, no trees shielded the streets from the heat during the day, so it took most of the night before the concrete, asphalt, and bricks cooled off.

We asked Tom and Dora about the group's comment that they lived too far apart. (The different families were scattered around the city and had to drive to be together.)

"We feel a great need to be closer together," Tom affirmed. "We're planning to move to the section called Germantown where the Gishes and Masts already live. We've begun the red tape of buying a house just around the corner from the

Masts, and the Wrights are bidding on a house next to them."

"The area will be similar to this one," said Dora. "But it's going to be harder for me. I'm from Argentina, so fitting into this Spanish neighborhood wasn't too hard, even though it really is a ghetto and very depressing. But the area we're moving to is changing from white to black, so we'll be far more in the center of change.

"I don't feel capable of dealing with the forces and tensions that kind of a situation creates—not on my own. It's only in community that I'd even attempt such a thing."

The ice cubes melted as fast as we added them to the water we were sipping. But finally we decided to try to sleep. Tom and Dora insisted we use their bed. It was on the top floor, away from their children who were having trouble sleeping. "Besides," Dora insisted, "if a breeze should come up, it'll blow through there first."

Tom pulled out an old window fan and said we could use it if we could figure a way to set it up. "I'm just not handy," he admitted. "That window sill is starting to rot a little, and I'm afraid the fan would fall out and hit someone on the head if I didn't mount it securely."

I temporarily set up the fan.

As sleep closed in, I thought drowsily, *It'll be good when this fellowship lives closer together . . . just even for a little reason . . . Art Gish just happens to be a carpenter along with the other gifts God has given him . . . .*

Part 5

God's Will in Community

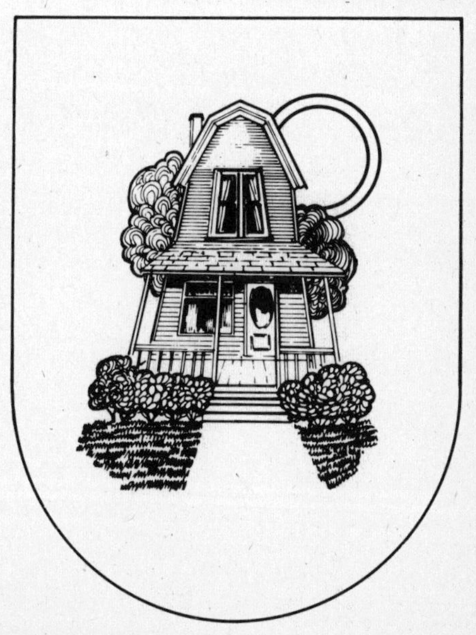

11

Discerning God's Will

(DAVE)

During our first year of experimenting with community life, we confined decision-making to the practical matters that obviously involved the group. We hammered out ways of getting the work done, using cars, figuring how much money to spend on food, and whether to buy some new garbage cans. I suppose it was the prospect of always having to have a meeting over such incidental things that partially scared some of our friends away from attempting community life. They were interested in the good company but not the cost and sacrifices.

At times we wondered whether our friends who were living alone weren't wisest. These doubts grew as we began to realize that the practical decisions weren't the only ones that affected the whole group. Many so-called personal decisions had their mutual repercussions. For instance, whether a person wanted to own a dog would seem a private matter. But it was nearly impossible for anyone else to have one since we hadn't been able to teach our own dog, Teak, what the Bible says about pacifism.

Or take the day one member of our household decided to get a car. He wanted one and thought he could afford it, so who were we to question his decision? But our driveway couldn't hold another car. His decision resulted in the hassle of car juggling when someone wanted to back out the driveway. It seems insignificant, but it was a daily interruption about which we had no say.

We wanted a second child and thought about adopting, but even that was not totally a private decision because everyone would have adjustments to make. Why should we complicate our life by involving so many others?

Then we started hearing other Christian communities talking about group decision-making and discernment of the will of God in the same sentence, as though they were the same thing.

Our thinking did a tailspin: group process to determine God's will? Not just for the group, but for each one within it? Committing "private" decisions to my brothers and sisters before the Lord?

As other areas came into focus, we caught a glimpse of the implications that living in a common or Body life might have on our private decisions and private futures. Our decisions did affect others. Small decisions in the past had big consequences for the present and future. If we wanted to do God's will, we would have to coordinate our lives with the rest of the members of His Body. How we spent our time, where we lived and worked—all affected how we exercised our gifts.

Some of the mystery of Christ's Body began to make sense. Paul had said, "Christ . . . is the head. Under his control all the different parts of the body fit together . . . . So when each separate part works as it should, the whole body grows and builds itself up through love" (Ephesians 4:15,16 Today's English Version).

"Christ's Body" had always been a familiar phrase to me because Scripture mentions it so often. I knew it referred to the believers, the church. But what did it mean?

The most dramatic expression of God's love for us came when He dwelt among us in the form of His Son, sent to live on earth in a human body. But that was only one phase of incarnation. It's a sad mistake to think that God's incarnation among men ended when Christ returned to be with the Father. God still lives among us. But now instead of being confined to a single physical body, He lives through the Holy Spirit in each believer. When believers consciously gather together in His name, Christ is incarnated in their midst in the new "Body of Christ," the church. (See Matthew 18:20.)

This all-important concept has been intellectually accepted throughout history by most orthodox Christian groups. But its application has often been twisted on the one hand into the popery of the Roman Catholic Church and on the other into the individualistic Christianity of the fundamentalists so that the assembled believers are stripped of any authority, and each believer becomes only vertically responsible to God.

Even the denominations in between aren't necessarily any clearer on the meaning of Christ's present incarnation. But throughout history, when Christian groups from across the denominational spectrum have understood what the present Body of Christ meant, they've been transformed. When their consciousness was raised about what they constituted as a group, their lives became exciting and powerful.

I started seeing why many of the more experienced church-communities considered decision-making the act of discerning God's will. And I began to see why few, if any, personal decisions fail to affect my brothers and sisters or my function as a member of the Body.

If only each of us could be absolutely certain that he was tuned into the leading of Christ our Head, we would always be fully coordinated.

My background was close to the fundamentalist end of the spectrum where church life was sometimes not much more than a coalition of Christians who got together because they held the same views on a list of doctrinal points. My own private ability to understand the Scriptures, weigh the advice of other Christians, evaluate the circumstances, and hear the "still, small voice" was my highest court in determining God's will for my life.

But the process was seldom satisfactory. I lacked the certainty needed for power. I observed in my own life and the lives of many Christian friends that often selfish ambitions, prejudice, or fear created a filter that distorted the true hue of God's leading. The Lord redeemed my mistakes and continued to teach me, but they were still mistakes.

An example occurred during our first community experiment with Jan and Gary Havens. When I was faced with a job change, I took matters into my own hands and, with a little help from Neta, tried to guide us through that crisis. Though I was not consciously rebellious to God's leading, I was in poor condition to hear His instructions correctly. Fear and bewilderment caused me to grab the first enticing job option that came along, though it meant our little community had to break up. We learned a lot from that mistake, but it's since been made clear that if we had trusted our Body, small as it was, the Lord would have shown us a better way, a less painful way.

In contrast to this was the answer the Philadelphia Fellowship gave us when we asked them what they would do if one of their members was transferred, say, to the West Coast. They said, "First we'd try to test if that was the job the Lord had for the person. If we agreed, we'd next ask if the Lord was telling the whole community (nine adults plus children) to move west, too. The possibility of breaking up would be low on our list, certainly not our first presumption."

That attitude says a lot about how they see themselves. They are not free-lance Christians. They constitute a local expression of the Body of Christ, and though God may ask them to send a member to the West Coast, he would never run off by himself. If he were supposed to go, his church would confirm his leading and commission him to go, possibly to start a new Body or join himself to one already existing.

At first, I thought this process of corporate decision-making had the obvious wisdom of a board of directors of a corporation. For a long time business has known that the pooled advice of several was better than the judgment of one person. But the more I talked to people at Reba Place and other communities, the more I saw that something far more exalted was going on. They believed that when they gathered in Christ's name, He was fleshed out in their midst, and that He would provide His specific direction for their group. These people went to decision-making meetings with a great sense of awe. It was one of their most sacred and important gatherings; they were there to hear God speak and conduct His business.

How different from the boring parliamentary harangues and power struggles of many church business meetings!

Decision-making in the church-community does not mean each person abdicates his own responsibility, as sometimes happens in a hierarchical church structure of bishops, archbishops, and popes. Each person is fully responsible. On the other hand, the individual need not carry the awesome weight of discovering God's will alone. He has the Body of Christ in which he can test what he thinks God is saying.

12
The State of Consensus

(DAVE)

If the life of Christ's local Body is not going to be spastic, with one foot going one way and the other flipping out another way, we must receive the messages from Christ our Head clearly and agree on them.

This condition of fully coordinated consensus is what Luke described in Acts 4:32 TEV: "The group of believers was one in mind and heart." While they were in this state, the next verse says: "With great power the apostles were giving witness to the resurrection of the Lord Jesus, and abundant grace was upon them all."

Their complete agreement reveals that the Holy Spirit actually resides within and can affect each believer. But it also takes into account that by himself, the believer can ignore or misinterpret the Spirit's leading. The Body, therefore, gives witness and substance to God's presence and leading.

As we studied the Scriptures with some consciousness of the meaning of Christ's Body, several other passages came alive. For instance, the authority Christ imparted to His followers began to make sense to me. "If two of you agree on earth about anything that they may ask, it shall be done for them by My Father who is in heaven. For where two or three have gathered together in My name, there I am in their midst" (Matthew 18:19,20).

It had seemed unlikely to me that Christ was rubber-stamping all future actions of groups calling themselves a "church." But it seemed plausible that assembled believers could know His will with assurance and then exercise it with authority. If a group prayerfully sought His will, the Spirit could use the checks and balances of the different believers to insure that when full agreement (not compromise) was finally reached, it would be God's will.

In the verse referred to above, Christ was teaching on the delicate matter of excommunication. No question seems more weighty, yet Christ left that frightening authority not to a disciplinary official, but to the assembly of the church.

This need for consensus in establishing God's authority is supported elsewhere. Paul recommends excommunication for a person involved in incest at the Corinthian church. But though Paul claims the right of apostleship, he makes his recommendation in recognition of Christ's teaching. "As you meet together," wrote Paul, "and I meet with you in my spirit, by the power of our Lord Jesus present with us, you are to hand this man over to Satan" (1 Corinthians 5:4,5 TEV). Paul was clear about what was to be done, but he recognized that the source of authority was to be finally channeled through the assembled believers.

The potential errors of free-lance Christians are contrasted with this ability of an enlightened Body in another event in the early church.

Some men had gone uncommissioned from Jerusalem up to Antioch and had begun teaching the Gentiles that they had to be circumcised to be saved. When the Jerusalem church heard about this, "the apostles and elders, together with the whole church, decided to choose some men from the group and send them to Antioch with Paul and Barnabas. They chose Judas, called Barsabbas, and Silas, two men who were highly respected by the brothers. They sent the following letter with them: 'The apostles and the elders, your brothers, send their greetings to all brothers of Gentile birth who live in Antioch and Syria and Cilicia. We have heard that some men of our group went out and troubled and upset you by what they said; they did not, however, receive any instructions from us to do this. And so we have met together and have all agreed to choose some messengers and send them to you. They will go with our dear friends Barnabas and Paul, who have risked their lives in the service of our Lord Jesus Christ. We send you, then, Judas and Silas who will tell you in person the same things we are writing. For the Holy Spirit and we have agreed not to put any other burden on you . . ." (Acts 15:22-28 TEV).

The authority emanated from the united body, and it was in their agreement that they were certain of the Holy Spirit's direction.

The condition of consensus is what Paul encouraged in Ephesians 4:3,4 TEV—"Do your best to preserve the unity which the Spirit gives, by the peace that binds you together. There is one body and one Spirit, just as there is one hope to which God has called you."

13
Deciding in Unity

(DAVE)

What breaks unity? If it is in unity that God's will is confirmed, how is full agreement maintained as a group of Christians confronts a problem and arrives at a decision?

If we view consensus as a state of mind and heart that exists between people before any decision is attempted, we can understand some of the basic forces that break unity.

One night Virgil Vogt from Reba Place Fellowship explained three conditions to us which cancel out unity before any decision is attempted. "Complete unity of mind and heart does not exist in a group if some members are not believers and therefore do not have the Holy Spirit in them. By definition they have something else going even though their paths may often cross those of Christ's Body."

The same is true to a large extent, Virgil told us, if the group includes people who may believe, but who have not fully committed themselves. If they have divided loyalties—if they are serving themselves or some other interest—how will they unscramble their signals? Of course even the committed have to deal with impure motives and temptations of the flesh, but if a person has consciously renounced other interests, he's at least not openly maintaining false gods.

And finally Virgil said, "If you cannot listen to your brother, you cannot listen to the Holy Spirit." He went on to explain that at times within a fellowship an unresolved conflict stands between members. They need to clear that up before they attempt any business. If they can't, they should abstain from the search for God's will on other matters until they can. The same is true, of course, of one person if he is out of fellowship with the Lord over some private matter.

Of course, God is not confined to such a quiet, attentive audience to make Himself heard. We are all aware of times when we have correctly heard His clear leading without the involvement of others to verify it. And we've also had times when God smashed through all kinds of distraction to get our attention. But those times are often more painful than we'd care to repeat.

Once a foundation of unity is established, we can follow some wise principles to discover or affirm the Holy Spirit's leading. The Quakers understood and practiced some of these ways in their meetings. For instance, when trying to decide whether to do one thing or another, we should gather all of the available facts. However, we might mistakenly seek to discover the Spirit's leading by adding up the pros and cons and then selecting the higher total. Rather, the "facts" should be understood as fully as possible by everyone and then set on the back burner, so to speak. The decisions should be made with an awareness of the facts and their consequences but not solely because of them.

Decisions based on facts alone risk the error of overlooking some unknown point that would have reversed the score had it been known. God, of course, is aware of all and can reveal the right course if we will wait in silent patience.

The real objective is to listen carefully for what the Holy Spirit is saying. He may lead contrary to the available facts. But He implants a certain peace in each person's heart to bear witness when we have selected the right path. And he will trouble some of us with a certain restlessness, a feeling that something is not quite right yet, if we have heard Him incorrectly. (We should note that deficient communication can produce a similar unease which is not the Spirit speaking. We can rectify it by clearing up misunderstandings.)

This whole way of life arises from the belief that God has not forsaken us, that He has sent us another Comforter, that He is the same yesterday, today, and forever. Since Moses, God has revealed His will to His people in two ways: His established, written Word as a standard, and the more detailed leading of His daily presence. The Law written on stone, and the cloud and pillar of fire. The Pentateuch, but also the judges and prophets. The whole Old Testament, but also the

Word made flesh in Christ. Today we have the entire record of Scripture, *and* the Holy Spirit.

One purpose of God's written record for us is to provide a standard against which we can evaluate daily direction. The Israelites knew the Old Testament prophets to be false if their statements contradicted the Law. We know Christ to be the promised Messiah partly because He fulfilled the prophecies concerning Him.

All things must be in agreement with the Bible. It is our first evaluator of truth. And in the Bible Christ said, "When He, the Spirit of truth comes, He will guide you into all truth" (John 16:13). In the detailed areas of our lives we can expect the Holy Spirit to direct us. God *is* interested! The Spirit's role as guide did not end when the apostles completed the canon.

When we were at Church of the Redeemer in Houston, the importance of the Bible in the process of discovering God's will was strongly emphasized. I was visiting a pastoral counseling session when the counselee said he felt God was telling him such and such. The counselor responded, "I'm sorry, but you are tuned to the wrong signals. That message clearly contradicts what the Bible says. The Bible is our standard. We have a great deal of latitude for application within its directives, but when the Bible is not used as the first test of truth, we risk getting so far off the track we couldn't hear if God shouted."

In my mind, that bit of advice provided a good check for any group feeling its oats over the power of Christ in its midst. Since our God is not one of contradiction and confusion, we can be certain that His will has not been discovered or validated if there is disagreement first with Scripture and then with the gathered believers.

When the members disagree, it is often because the Spirit wants to reveal another alternative. When the problem is first laid out, we often think there are only two ways to go. But when we can't reach clarity on one of those ways, the Spirit may want us to keep exploring until another way is found—His way.

In spite of the spiritual dynamics (the search for the leading of the Spirit) people commonly fear that the group process will ignore the autonomy of the individual. But as Art Gish of the Philadelphia Fellowship pointed out, "The condition of consensus is different than compromise. Compromise is often nothing more than the lowest common denominator on which men can agree. And it is frequently far removed from the true desires of everyone, especially the minority opinion."

No voluntary organization can force a person to do something against his will over a long period of time. A disgruntled minority will ultimately split away from the group or destroy it. For the church-community operating in unity, the individual is even more sacred than in a democracy. Democracies consistently violate the will of the minority; the only alternatives are, "Love it or leave it." The sole requirement in the church-community is that everyone be honestly searching for and ready to do God's will. Attitude is the only question.

This mix of responsibility and submission is something few Christians are prepared for. My church background had taught me personal responsibility, but had given me a fear of submitting to anyone else. Someone from a hierarchical church background may have practice in submitting, but not in being personally, actively involved in searching out God's will. Maintaining unity in a church-community demands the ability and willingness to do both. I need to take active and personal responsibility for discovering God's leading, and I need to involve other believers on a determining level in that process. People can resolve this paradox of responsibility and submission in a situation where they believe in the Holy Spirit's leading.

The group needs to remember, however, that in personal matters a mature person's initial response will often express the leading of the Spirit. In fact, we should expect that with increased spiritual maturity, a person will conform more and more to the image of Christ until his first desires are almost always Christ's. But because we are still human we will always be capable of ignoring and distorting God's leading. Therefore, the group's primary function is to test or validate those personal leadings.

It's overwhelming to be in a meeting where God's will is being searched out in a serious manner. Many times a miracle occurs. I've found it mind-blowing to approach a decision with a logical rationale for a solution, only to have my opinion melt and become twice as confident over a new solution. Sometimes I can't analyze how I moved from one point to another, but when the affair is over, it becomes obvious that God's way revealed in unity was the only way things could have worked.

14
Leadership and Authority

(DAVE)

When we first visited Church of the Redeemer, almost everything about the authority structure collided with my will. Moments after we had arrived at the Hansen household where we were to stay after a day-long, hot ride in the car, our three-year-old Julian had to go to the bathroom. I rushed out of the upstairs bedroom where I had just set down two big suitcases, grabbed his hand, and ran down the hall. (We were still responding like firemen when he called, hoping to reinforce our recent successes at potty training.) The bathroom we found was occupied, so we wheeled around and ran down the back stairs, emerging in the kitchen. To someone I hadn't met yet I said, "Is there another bathroom? Julian has to go and someone's using the upstairs one."

The man responded, "Yeah, right behind you and around the corner. It's a good thing you didn't use the upstairs bathroom," he called after us. "It's the girls', and men aren't to go in it. This one down here is for men."

"Wow, who was that?" I wondered as I fumbled at Julian's pants buttons after slipping in and closing the door. (We made it in time.) "Maybe they have some problem with bathroom invaders," I mused.

When I came out, the direction-giver introduced himself. He was head of the household, Bob Hansen. And for the next couple of days, I got the feeling that "head of the household" superseded his name. We were told where to sit and when to sit and that Julian made too much noise at the table. Oh yes, we were given one concession: we were allowed to continue as the sole disciplinarians of Julian. "Usually," Bob explained, "the head of the household takes over the role of chief disciplinarian for everyone under his roof."

Rebellion began boiling inside me, and Neta wasn't far behind. By the second night we'd built up a head of steam big enough to power a locomotive halfway across Texas. And it blew! Neta left the table and went to our room in tears, and I started pinning Bob Hansen to the wall for every little bit of what I thought was arbitrary ax-wielding since we had arrived.

Strangely enough, Bob took it all. He genuinely apologized for the way a few things had come across, explained a few others so I realized it had been *I* who had been judgmental and had judged wrongly. And then he went on to a couple of points where I had thought he had been most arbitrary, and briefly justified his actions by stating, "That's what God wanted me to do."

At first that was hard to take—bringing God in on his side. Later I had to eat turkey as several things proved to have a purpose and worked out right.

To top off my tirade, he invited me to visit their elders' meeting that night. I had expected him to direct me out the door and down the street, and we'd happily have gone.

But how could he trust me in a meeting of their inner circle?

At that meeting I began to see why Bob had invited me. He had faith that the Holy Spirit would make it evident that God's work was being done there at Church of the Redeemer.

The meeting of about twenty-four elders of the community of more than four hundred people was a model of consensus. The group was clearly of one mind and spirit. Every point that arose was dealt with in that profoundly patient way of discovering the Holy Spirit's leading on the issue and making sure that every elder was certain it was the right thing to do. They never left a question in anyone's mind, and I could see there would never be an I-told-you-so.

Once, during the meeting when they seemed unable to agree on a decision, one of the elders said, "I hear a lot of opinions being expressed. People are saying, 'Well, I think this, and I think that.' I wonder if we shouldn't be a little bit more deliberate about discovering the Lord's opinion. We're not here to parley our personal opinions, are we? Ego-tripping just wastes our time. Before we blurt out something, let's just ask ourselves whether we think we are expressing the Holy Spirit or some selfish spirit."

That little exhortation reined in the group like a runaway horse. In only a few minutes they came to clarity on the issue. It didn't intimidate people. I watched; every person continued to participate. But the mood was different, and as an observer, I could tell that the quality of each person's input was different.

On one issue they all agreed that they weren't ready to make a decision and needed to wait until the Lord brought about new developments. So they put it off until a later date.

During the meeting they laid hands on and commissioned two men to go to Colorado and begin a work of renewal in a parish church there, hoping they would awaken the people to a new relationship with the Holy Spirit, an understanding of themselves as Christ's Body and work of the church.

Once in discussing a point of business an elder suggested a direction to which no one seemed to have an immediate response. People didn't seem to be against it; it was just such a new direction in the discussion that no one seemed to know how to respond. Finally another elder asked, "Are you speaking that as from the Lord?"

The first elder thought carefully a few moments. "Yes, I believe I am," he said. And on the weight of that testimony and the fact that there was no "check," they all agreed to take the newly suggested direction as a direct leading from the Holy Spirit.

Check is the word that they used to describe a

point of objection that anyone had to a proposition. Sometimes when a person said he must check something, it was later discovered that his objection was human; he may not have been aware of some important information, or he may have been expressing wrong motives. If either of these were the case, further discussion usually brought him into agreement.

On the other hand a check may be the Holy Spirit saving the group from a serious mistake. This possibility seemed so important that I got the impression objections were welcomed and that no one was afraid to say that he must check something.

Much of the meeting was spent evaluating every detail of the previous praise and teaching service. These services were Redeemer's main occasions for communicating the gospel to the neighborhood. Twice a week these meetings drew in as many as twelve hundred people—many obviously not part of the church. The way the gospel was presented at these services was understandably crucial. The spirit of the meetings, the participation of community members, the songs chosen, the way they were led and sung, the restlessness of people, the orderliness of the service and whether some message in an unknown tongue was immediately interpreted, the content and exact wording of the teaching—everything was of utmost importance. The elders' meeting tried to discover if the Holy Spirit would have it done differently next time.

The meeting began at five o'clock in the afternoon and finally ended at two A.M. The elders met at least twice a week, and they told me it was common for their meetings to last that late.

In spite of the hour I couldn't sleep when we returned to the Hansen household. Neta and I stayed up and talked. "Why," I puzzled, "if the elders understand the concept of consensus so well, doesn't the community practice it throughout? Since they were obviously so open to hearing the Spirit speak, why didn't He tell them to practice a more universal consensus throughout their community and within their households?"

The next day I began getting an answer to my question.

As I talked with community members, I began to discover that consensus did prevail. Everyone seemed to be in unity about what was happening. All members were confident that the Lord's will was being realized. They *were* of one mind and spirit.

I also discovered that the purpose God had for Redeemer had a great deal to do with the way they were set up. They were a ministering church, and their households were ministering households. Their structure reflected a situation necessary for larger groups that are open to growth. When many people are assimilated, the purity of purpose can be maintained only if leaders can provide sound guidance. It would also be thoughtlessly cruel to demand that an emotionally or mentally weak person assume the same degree of responsibility as a strong person. The same is true of a spiritually immature person. A brand new Christian with little knowledge of the Bible would be at a loss in testing things by biblical standards until he's had a chance to learn.

Church of the Redeemer took in drug addicts, alcoholics, people with messed-up marriages, the mentally and emotionally ill, and people with any number of other serious problems. Only one thing was required of them—that they submit to the authority of the Lord Jesus Christ in their midst. Even the non-Christian was received if he accepted what they could offer. Such people were, of course, not members, but the Christians at Redeemer realized that sin could make a person so sick that he was in no condition to understand what a lifelong commitment to Christ amounted to. Skid-row derelicts, for instance, would say yes to anything for a bowl of soup. But it might take weeks before they could make an intelligent and lasting decision for Christ.

This order of authority in their church enabled them to be the channel for healing many people because they had a place for people no matter what their level of maturity in the Lord. Bob Hansen pointed out to me that the objective of ministry was to help each believer grow into the full stature of Christ. This, however, scarcely meant that each person was destined to be a leader. Leadership was a gift to be used in service for building up the body, as with all other gifts. It was not merely equivalent to greater maturity; a leader had to be mature, but most mature Christians were not leaders. They had other gifts. This was important to understand to avoid pride and jealousy. Christians were servants only, obligated to use the gift the Holy Spirit had seen fit to give for service to Christ's Body.

Since our visit in Houston we have discovered that most of the larger, more established communities recognize the need and biblical appropriateness of leadership. Leaders are not selected by a popularity contest, nor is leadership conferred by human authority. It is a gift given by the Holy Spirit. The role of a group is to recognize and identify what He gives.

It seems important that leaders remember the attitude of service for the Body so that they avoid the trap of lording their responsibilities over others. In an attempt to promote this consciousness, the Society of Brothers had leaders they call "Servants of the Word."

I talked to Bob Hansen about this, because it still bothered me how strongly we had clashed at the first. I would have never guessed he was my servant or anybody else's. I had learned a lot about leadership and was willing to accept the call for it in the Bible and the appropriateness of it in the community, but what had happened those first couple of days?

"It may have been the unfortunate expression of our fallen human natures," said Bob. "But I believe God redeemed it. In fact, it may have been that He providentially planned it. We don't think that anything here happens by accident."

I thought about that. We were able to remain in Houston only a little over a week. We could have been guests in any number of other households, but we ended up in the Hansen household where Bob's strong personality and mine clashed from the beginning. Had we gone elsewhere, we would probably not have dealt with the question of leadership, authority, and submission. The flavor of the community would have bothered us, but with someone else it may not have come out in the open. We would probably have smouldered during the whole time and gone away bitter and confused.

As it was, my resistance to authority came to a head early, and dealing with it brought far more understanding of the need for leadership. As we look back over our trip, that was obviously the most important thing for us to learn in Houston.

If we ever return, we'll be happy to visit the Hansen household.

Part 6

The Family in Community

15

Who Is the Family?

(NETA)

The Mosley trailer stood between the peanut field and the sewing industry building at Koinonia. Mediterranean-style furniture and an antique organ made the inside an un-trailer-like surprise. Don Mosley, lanky and friendly, was baby-sitting his three-year-old son while his pregnant wife Carolyn attended one of the weekend sessions with the Trappist monk visiting Koinonia. Don was up to his elbows in dish suds when I knocked on the trailer door, so while Julian and Tony scrambled for the toys, I dried dishes and we talked.

"We didn't come to Koinonia because we felt any particular need in our family life," he said in response to my inquiries. "We saw it mainly as a way to put our beliefs into practice by ministering to the poor. In fact, we have less family time together than before. I put in more than an eight-hour day in getting the housing villages ready for people to move in, keeping the houses in repair, and doing carpentry and maintenance around the farm."

The two little boys had disappeared to ride tricycles along the path through the peanut fields, and Don peered out the trailer window to keep them in sight. "But it's good for my family here," he continued emphatically. "When the parents are whole people, involved in meaningful work, it's good for the children, too. One of the ways we've changed most is that we've loosened up our concept of the tight-knit little family spending all its time together; we've brought other people into our family circle."

Some people find it hard to accept that concept. In our fragmented society, it's understandable that the family is fighting to survive. Fathers commute an hour each way into the city; children and parents, husbands and wives live in different spheres of activities and involvement; families are isolated from close friends and relatives by job transfers and think that their complex needs should be met from within. Whatever combination might be pulling them apart may make them cry out, "We need more time together!" It's as if the family can think only in terms of one solution: huddle closer together as a family, shut everyone and everything else out, recover strength to face the battle once again.

There's a vast difference between family members flying in different directions trying to meet their needs and drawing other people into the concept of family to meet those needs. In spite of Don Mosley's long workday at Koinonia, several factors affected the quality of their family life. For one, the Mosleys lived and worked in the same place. As Carolyn and Tony walked from the trailer to one of the other buildings on an errand, they might see Don building a porch for one of the cottages, and they'd wave, maybe even stop and chat. The dinner bell always brought Don together with his family in the farm's dining room. If the family had an important errand in town, Don could rearrange his work to be with them. If a babysitter were needed for Tony, it was someone he knew, someone he saw every day, "one of the family."

At a Bible study at Church of the Redeemer in Houston, a community member said, "People today have a false view of what the family is all about—its separateness, its sacredness that can't be broken into. But the Bible says to love your brother as much as your wife and children." The alternative to the fragmented family is not the isolated family but the *integrated* family—integrated into the place, work, service, and relationships that God has for that family.

The family needs more than just time together. The individual family was never meant to carry the load it's now trying to carry. The small family of mother, father, and children needs a larger supportive context. It thrives best in the give and take of a closely knit community of families that are sensitive to each other's needs and willing to give and receive the resources each has to offer. Where this is not present and the family tries to face all the problems of human existence by itself, frustration takes over, or perhaps the family simply rides with the tide of mass opinion that says, "Marriage and the family are doomed."

Jesus set an example of the attitude the Christian is to have. Once, while He was seated in the middle of His disciples, His mother and brothers came wanting to take Him home. Jesus responded by saying, "Who is my mother and who are my brothers?" And then looking around at his disciples He said, "Behold, My mother and My brothers! For whoever shall do the will of My Father who is in heaven, he is My brother and sister and mother" (Matthew 12:48-50). Jesus was not excluding His family but including those who were involved with Him intimately, daily seeking and doing the will of God.

In my childhood, I remember feeling quite disgruntled toward church activities and "Christian service" responsibilities that took my parents away from home so many evenings. Even in the first few years of married life, we had a struggle with Christian organizations we worked for because they demanded overtime and energy at the expense of family life. I felt that if "serving the Lord" meant neglecting one's family, it brought Him no honor.

When I first visited Church of the Redeemer in Houston and its vast ministries, I had trouble at first understanding the demands placed on a few persons that took them away from their families for weeks at a time, or that involved one or more members of the family long hours into the evening "doing the Lord's work."

But I was looking at the situation with a limited perspective on Christian community. There *is* work to be done in God's Kingdom which demands time and energy of certain persons apart from the family. However, suppose a community of Christians determines that a person should do God's work in a way that leaves him less free to meet needs within the family. Then it becomes the concern of the community to give that family the additional support and daily resources it needs. This is one reason for the existence of ministering extended households. On the other hand, the community might discern that a person should spend *more* time with his family; then they should take the necessary steps to make that possible. The most important factor is that the community and the individual have a sense that each person is doing what he should be doing in the Body, and that all the important needs of individuals and families are being met.

Many of the communities we visited integrated activities and responsibilities so that the children were linked up with the daily work of the parents. In some communities this took the form of a common work close to the daily life of other family members. Elsewhere, if a parent held a job out in the larger society, the community looked after the children and kept the number of activities in balance so that parents were able to spend quality time with their families. At Reba Place Fellowship, for example, living within walking distance of each other allows parents to spend time with their family and put younger ones to bed before going to a fellowship meeting.

The beauty of community is that all aspects of life—job, family, school, worship, activities, ministry, fellowship—are the active concern of the whole community, to be integrated into a meaningful whole. It's not a magic formula. Each community must deal with its own situation and the particular needs of the families involved. As needs change, the community must continue to deal with them conscientiously, seeking God's will.

16
Husbands and Wives

(NETA)

What effect does community have on marriage?

Opening up the marriage relationship

Dave and I had been moving toward the concept of a Christian extended-family household when Julian was born. All else faded in the first elation of loving and caring for that tiny, sturdy little boy. Then my mother flew home, Dave plunged once more into his work—and there I was, cornered in a one-bedroom house with a baby who did only three things: sleep, cry, and nurse.

By the time Dave returned each evening, I was starving for someone to listen to me, talk to me, and involve me in something more than changing diapers and deciding what to cook for dinner. I missed the stimulation of the magazine office where I'd worked, the ideas being whacked around, the daily contact with people. I was secretly afraid I would cease to grow as a person and be unable to keep up with Dave's involvement with the outside world.

"What did you do today?" I queried Dave the minute he came through the door. "Who did you see? What did they say? What did you say? What happened then? What did you think about?" Dave coped as best he could for a few weeks, but gradually he moved toward the good-grief,-leave-me-alone stage.

It all seems a bit humorous now, but at the time we realized a significant fact: husbands and wives aren't able to meet *all* of each other's needs. In our case I simply needed adult companionship on a daily basis now that I was home with a nursing baby. I couldn't continue to live vicariously through Dave; it wasn't fair to him or me.

Added to the reasons why we were seeking Christian community, this was the final straw that led us to expand our family. Julian was three months old when we found a huge old house and signed a lease with Jan and Gary Havens and their five-month-old Kathy.

The most immediate joy of an extended household for me was companionship during the day. Not a pack-up-the-baby-and-drive-two-miles-to-see-somebody companionship, but a just-being-there companionship. Jan and I were able to talk out baby-care frustrations, give each other a helping hand; one of us could take over for an hour so the other could have time to herself; we could share thoughts with another adult mind, help each other keep the minor tragedies of a baby's first year in perspective.

Did this mean I didn't need Dave? That I shared with Jan what I should have shared with Dave? That he was left out of my daily struggles and joys?

No. His reaction after the first week was, "It's so great to come home to a wife who's not frustrated out of her wits!" Because Jan and I shared the cooking, Dave, Julian, and I often had a leisurely hour to enjoy each other before supper. Because of Jan's help, I had time to read, write, or just get out, and I began to feel part of the world again, with ideas to share with Dave and others. We could be genuinely interested in each other's day without being warped by my loneliness and frustration.

Opening up our lives and sharing them helped meet needs we hadn't thought of. For instance, Gary's job regularly took him away for a few days. It was comforting to him to know Jan and the baby were taken care of in case something happened; and it was a lot more pleasant for Jan not to be all alone for those few days.

This raises a problem: a husband or wife may feel threatened if a spouse needs other people. I feel the marriage relationship is unique, and the deepest of all relationships—but it's a fallacy to think it satisfies every human need. The way our society is structured, wives and husbands are often separated for many hours of each day, and the spouse at home (still usually the wife, in spite of women's lib) has only superficial contact with other friends or adults. The spouse who works outside the home and comes in contact with more people hardly fares better; those contacts may still be superficial. Even having company for dinner or visiting at another couple's house usually fails to provide supportive relationships with others.

We should not confuse the uniqueness and sexual exclusiveness of Christian marriage with possessiveness. Possessiveness in marriage grows out of jealousy, selfishness, or fear. An unpossessive attitude isn't a care-less attitude, a you-go-your-way-I'll-go-mine kind of freedom. Rather, it frees each partner from trying to meet each other's needs totally; it frees each to have supportive relationships with other Christian brothers and sisters and to minister to others as well.

Both the purpose and structure of Christian community provide supportive relationships for the married couple, both together and as individuals. Whether a person lives in an extended- or single-family household isn't as important as the intent of the community to meet the needs of each person. The nearness of people in the community is an important factor; so are group sharing and decision-making meetings, which provide each person an opportunity to make his needs known.

Living more recently in the extended household of Common Circle has made it possible for both Dave and me to enjoy the friendship of the opposite sex easily and naturally as brothers and sisters. Before living in an extended household, I would have felt odd walking Dave Moberg to the train just for a time to talk. I wouldn't have had the opportunity to learn guitar from Toht in the evenings while Dave planned an organic garden with equally enthusiastic Becky or argued politics with Sharon. We both realize how much these relationships have enriched us, and how lopsided our lives would be if we had continued to limit our friendships outside our marriage only to "the girls" for me or "the guys" for him.

Strengthening the marriage relationship

Community also nurtures the relationship between the two married persons themselves. Some relationships are insecure or troubled (maybe all are at one time or another) and need to be treated cautiously, both by the couple involved and the other community members.

Russ and Pat Harris at Reba Place Fellowship, for instance, were having some tensions in their marriage. Pat said, "Our small group discerned that we needed time to work on our family life. It was true. We'd each been concentrating on ourselves, getting right with the Lord in areas we'd been holding back from Him, but not tackling problems concerning our relationship with each other and with our children." They had to face such things as taking each other for granted, not trusting each other, arguing quite a bit.

With the suggestions and prayerful support of their small group, Russ and Pat set aside time each week just for each other, to build up their relationship. Because they were in an environment of people who cared about them and their marriage, the Harrises couldn't suppress their problems, pretending they didn't exist.

The extended-family household is often asked questions about whether it's "proper" for married couples to live in the same house together or with single persons—or less subtly, "Isn't sex a problem?" We reply immediately that it's basic for Christians in community to hold a common belief in the rightness and uniqueness of the marriage relationship as God ordained it—one man and one woman becoming one flesh. With this common commitment, the extended family becomes a practical, not a moral, question.

One practical question that often comes up is whether an extended-family household offers enough privacy for a marriage relationship. Some friends of ours outside community swear they need the whole house as their private quarters and could never live with other people. Maybe so, if the house is very small. But relatively few people throughout history or even today have needed the exclusive space Americans seem to think they need. Note that I'm not criticizing the need for space, but *exclusive* space.

It's safe to say that private space and private time are important to some degree for every couple (and for single persons too). We function well at Common Circle with two connected bedrooms for the three of us Jacksons, and share two baths, a study, a living room, a dining room, a kitchen, and a basement with the other five members of our household. Dave and Becky Toht, the other married couple, need another private room as a study and art room, and we'd like to make this possible.

At Fairview Mennonite House in Wichita, Kansas, a one-household community of seventeen persons, the old three-story house was remodeled to give each family private quarters on the second and third floors. Each section included bedrooms and a bathroom for each family. The attic was used for common storage and a library; the first floor was common space. Said one mother of three boys, "We've never had so much space!"

We admit it, we don't run around the house without our clothes on at night as we used to do when we lived in an apartment by ourselves. We might miss that, except we feel it's a small freedom to give up for what we have gained by living in an extended household.

Paper-thin walls wouldn't make an ideal house for an extended household—or for a single family with children, for that matter. Rules need to be laid down about respecting closed doors and knocking before entering a bedroom (although we've never had to mention any such thing because it's just understood).

The needs of a couple differ from time to time as well. Here at Common Circle, Dave and Becky Toht are feeling they need some extra time and space for their relationship for a while after Dave finishes school next spring. Both Dave and Becky recognize the benefits of the extended household and have contributed much. They can see their present need for a separate dwelling changing in the future. But all of us recognize their present need as valid, so as a group we are working to make it possible for them to have the option of an apartment to themselves in the context of community.

When a married couple first lives in community, and especially in an extended household, they experience a normal tension about quarreling with each other within earshot of others. It's tempting to want to hide our disagreements from others, to protect the mask we often wear on our marriage. In one sense this tension has a healthy effect. One young husband said, "Living with another couple in the house makes me think twice before shooting off my mouth at my wife."

But hiding all disagreements and problems isn't always healthy. Husbands and wives can often benefit from the perspective and counsel of Christian brothers and sisters whom they love and trust.

We need to be accountable to Christ's Body for our marriage relationship, just as we are accountable for the use of our gifts, possessions, money, time, jobs—our very lives. This is the reality of committing our lives and relationships to Christ.

It's helped me to treat difficulties in our marriage relationship in the same order Jesus outlined for Christian brothers in Matthew 18:15-17. First, go to the person involved. This means I *always* go to my husband first with any disagreement or problem I have with him, and we try to work it out together. In most cases we can handle problems on this level because of our basic love and respect for each other. But sometimes we come to a stalemate, and we mutually agree to share the problem with the brothers and sisters who care about us. We have several times each week when this is appropriate—at our Tuesday morning sharing meeting, when we bring individual concerns for prayer, or at our weekly evening household meeting, when we devote time to discussion and decision.

Bringing a disagreement or problem to others

doesn't mean it has to be a major crisis; for us, it's helped us keep small problems small by giving us perspective and input on the question early.

Dave and I recently had a heated argument about child-rearing. Usually we work out these things by ourselves, but this time we really seemed to deadlock. We wanted to work it out, and knew we *had* to; we hated the distance it was creating between us. So we brought up our problem at our weekly household meeting.

Being able to talk about it but not having to direct our thoughts directly at each other helped us release some emotional tension. Then hearing other people verbalize the problem from their perspective took us out of the corners we'd backed ourselves into. I don't even remember what was finally said, but afterwards Dave and I were able to approach the matter once again in a loving way and come to a workable conclusion.

17

Single Persons

(NETA)

When we first thought about community and extended households, we didn't think in terms of single people. We thought working toward community would take a commitment young singles wouldn't make.

On the other hand, people who know little about community or who get their main image from the mass-media concept of the "commune" think of it *primarily* in terms of young single people. "Oh, you kids can do something interesting like that, but I'm too old for it." Their concept is that singles don't have family responsibilities, aren't committed to a job, can move around and experiment with life-styles, don't have to think in terms of security or stability.

Both concepts—only marrieds, only singles—are wrong.

One evening our household was talking about how we'd been challenged toward fuller community life: being a church, making an open-ended commitment of ourselves, our money and possessions, our future. "I'm afraid," I admitted, "that a decision toward fuller community would have different weight for married people than for singles. If we make that kind of commitment, we're putting the future of our child on the line along with our car, the furniture, and the appliances we've invested in. It seems to me that single people wouldn't have as much to consider or to lose."

Dave Moberg spoke up quietly. "There's another side to that, though. From my point of view, the important decision about whom to marry is already behind you. You've been able to buy a car and enjoy your furniture and appliances for awhile. But suppose I make the decision to commit myself to a full expression of community. Right away it affects and narrows some basic decisions for me, decisions you've been 'free' to make on your own."

Our terminology of "having as much to lose" and "being free to make decisions on our own" weren't accurate comments on the nature of full community, because the deepest meaning of Christian community puts the Christian in the freest, richest context of all—being absorbed fully into Christ's Body, seeking and doing His perfect will. But our words accurately betrayed some of our human fears and self concerns.

I thought a lot about what Dave had said.

Christian community doesn't depend on age or marriage status. God calls us where we are and asks us to give all that we have to Him and His Body. Single and married people may have different areas to commit, but the commitment from each must be total.

This kind of commitment has serious implications for the single person. Dave Moberg said, "If I'm serious about community, I immediately narrow the choice I have concerning a future wife. She has to be a girl who also feels that community is where she is supposed to be."

A young single girl in another small community expressed her feelings this way: "If I were considering marriage to someone, I'd share it with my brothers and sisters in Christ. After sufficient Bible study, prayer, and meditation, I'd expect God to help me understand His will by bringing us all into agreement about whether the answer was yes, no, or wait."

She added, "I could trust another person to help in this kind of decision only on one condition. I'd have to be confident that the person was as committed to discovering God's will for my life as for his own. To me, the practical sharing of money and possessions within our fellowship is a tangible reassurance of the commitment we share; it means people aren't pursuing the welfare of their own private futures. They aren't hoarding plans to skip out."

Jim Short, a solid blond-bearded member of Plow Creek Fellowship, felt that Christian community provided fullness for him as a single person. "Too many people marry," he insisted, "because they're lonely or bored; no one cares about them or shares in their life. But the Body of Christ should fulfill these needs for everyone, including singles. There shouldn't be any lonely, bored Christians. If a single person needs supportive relationships, community takes the pressure off so he doesn't jump at the first chance he gets for a marriage companion."

In a few communities we visited, single people lived in separate housing. But many integrated singles into family life. At the Society of Brothers, for instance, they had rooms of their own but each one, young or old, had a family he related to. Singles were included in family outings, the twice-a-week family suppers, daily breakfast, family time, birthday celebrations, and so forth.

One young man in a newly formed community, however, expressed discontent with being integrated into the child-care role as well. "Kids will come along soon enough," he said during a discussion on family life when the twenty communities got together at Reba Place. "Singles shouldn't have to handle that responsibility yet. I don't like being considered a handy baby-sitter."

People from the Society of Brothers didn't understand that attitude. "Caring for children is one of our chief joys," one single man responded. "Everyone counts it a special privilege if he's freed from some of the other responsibilties and gets to spend time with the kids."

We have a friend, an attractive editor, who lives in a small community that is growing toward extended households. She said, "I don't like being segregated out of normal family life just because I'm not married and don't have children of my own. What if I never get married? I love children, love the feel of a family around me. I would even like to work part-time and spend the rest working with the community children. I think this should be possible for the single person in Christian community."

Single people shouldn't be thought of as "handy baby-sitters." Nor should a community automatically separate a single life-style from a family life-style. Both extremes are demeaning and fail to take the individual needs of a single person into consideration. Each group should determine the needs of its single members and then work out a structure that meets them best.

It's unfortunate that our society has developed a mind-set that thinks (or worse, says), "If you're not married, something must be wrong with you." During our visits to various communities, we became aware that single people *as singles* in a household or community added a great deal. As Paul the Apostle said of himself in the New Testament, single people can do a work for the Lord and His Body that married persons often can't. Certain responsibilities and ministries need special gifts, time, and energy apart from family responsibilities. Even on the child-care level, I've noticed that single people often give a special quality of time to children just because they *don't* have the constant responsibility that parents have.

As one single at Reba Place Fellowship declared, "We should assume God calls us to be single unless He definitely calls us *out of* singleness into marriage." Not a common view today, but one worth hearing.

I personally lean strongly toward the concept of

the *extended family* where single persons, married couples, children, teens, grandparents, all ages and stages of life can be interrelated in a close and mutually beneficial way; this is superior to the distinct categories we now have in our society. The extended family used to be the norm for nearly all societies, including our own. Today the emerging Christian communities support this concept by bringing all sorts of people into a meaningful whole—learning from each other, using each one's particular gifts, meeting each one's particular needs. The concept of family, instead of being a category limited to parents and children, widens like the ripples from a pebble dropped in a pond: the biological family widens to the extended-household family which widens even further to the community family.

18

Men and Women: Roles and Relationships

(NETA)

Dave and several of the Memphis Fellowship men had just finished patching a leaky roof. This group, a one-household community in Memphis, Tennessee, was the first stop on our trip. About fourteen persons lived in the household, single except for two married couples and one child. The group was only about a year old and had grown out of a Bible study on the Christian life. A former Baptist minister provided teaching and counseling, while other members shouldered other leadership responsibilities. Our welcome had been warm, and the group seemed eager to hear and learn from other communities.

I sat down on the back steps and watched as the fellows put away the tools and cleaned the tar off their hands. Robbie Gaylor, a gentle-eyed twenty-year-old with a compelling grin, glanced up and said teasingly, *"You're* the woman I want to see."

"Sure," I grinned back. "What's on your mind?"

Still working on his hands with a rag, he sat down on the steps and said more seriously, "Do you have any experience with women who can't get along in the kitchen?"

I was surprised, but realized there might be more back of his question, so I said, "Well, our own situation is somewhat different from yours. You have two women responsible full-time for the kitchen, laundry, and housework. In our household everybody has a job, so we divide up both the housework and the cooking responsibilities. And with our particular schedules it makes sense for each person to do his own laundry."

"You think it's O.K. for the women to work at a job, then?"

"It's a decision that depends on the person and the situation," I answered. "I personally have strong feelings about parents being at home when children are small. I feel fortunate that I can do my work—writing and editing—at home. Dave also works at home, so we both share the care for Julian."

I thought a bit. "I don't feel the 'right to work' should be at the expense of a marriage, or that children should suffer. A community should help each person do what's best for him and for the group as a whole. This involves some give-and-take. The group shouldn't treat a person as a thing to 'do this' or 'do that'; neither should a person pursue his 'rights' or interests without considering the other people in the family and the group. Whether a woman *or* a man should work at a paying job should be decided for each individual, each situation, the particular needs of each group. I've sometimes felt that outside of community it's the *man* who needs liberating from a greedy wife who forces him to earn more and more money at a meaningless job! But to answer your question simply, I'd say yes, women working outside the home is a definite option."

"Someone from Reba Place Fellowship told me you can't deal with people as a group," Robbie mused, "lumping all women into the same role, for instance. You need to deal with people as individuals. One of our girls, Marge, was an X-ray technician before becoming a Christian and moving into community with her husband. When we were about a month old the group decided that rather than work she should care for the household. I didn't realize how much she enjoyed her job until recently, when she asked about going back. Some of the people here have strong feelings that she shouldn't, but I'm beginning to think she should. We have quite a bit of work around this household, but not enough to keep two women busy full-time. Amy, the other girl, is a real go-getter when it comes to housework, and a lot of times there just isn't that much left for Marge to do."

"Well," I said, "it's important to keep making decisions depending on what the situation is and how a person's needs change. Six months from now our household may share work differently, or Dave and I may work out a different relationship regarding child care."

Dave had joined us on the back steps now, and he spoke up. "I had to get adjusted to taking care of Julian part of each day. But I'm glad that was our decision, because it's been so rewarding for me to get to know him. And it's valuable for Julian to spend a sizable chunk of the day with each of us."

Robbie grinned. "Yeah, I've noticed how you do that—Dave putting Julian to bed one night, Neta the next. That's really beautiful. I like that."

"Living in community helps develop relationships between men and women in many ways," I said, thinking about how we'd been affected. "For instance, in community you don't have to be so fearsomely dependent on just one person to fulfill all your needs. Also, a person can have friends of both sexes more easily. I can relate to the people in our household in other ways than through my 'wife' role: I'm a person, a woman, a friend, a sister.

"And," I continued, "living in community can free both men and women to lead meaningful lives by providing more resources and making more options possible. For instance, Dave wanted to work on a book about his experience of becoming a conscientious objector, but free-lance writing is a pretty shaky way to make a living, especially at first. So he was able to choose to work at home because in community it's not so crucial to make *X* number of dollars, both because living in community is more resourceful, and because of our attitude of sharing."

The call for lunch came from inside the house.

Before we went in, Dave said, "If Marge and Amy aren't getting along as they work together in the household, you might explore two things. If that is what each of them should be doing, they should be able to confirm that within themselves as well and work on an attitude of really serving the others in the group through their work. However, maybe the group as a whole needs to explore its attitude toward women as individuals and whether their needs are being fully met."

The subject of men and women—their attitudes toward each other *as* men and women, and the roles they fulfill—is important in community. Three things primarily have affected our own attitudes in our marriage and toward other people: first, the intent of the community as a whole to meet the needs of each person, male and female; second, the attitude in community of serving each other in love in all that we do; and third, full submission to Christ, and thus to each other in His Body.

Before we lived in community, I had pretty much accepted the standard role of housekeeping and cooking even when I was working full-time. My biggest hang-up was not in the things I had to do, but in the arrangement of duties. Dave seemed to be able to come home, read the paper, and relax; I came home from work and immediately had to plunge into breakfast dishes plus supper and household chores.

Even when we first moved into an extended household with the Havenses, our roles were pretty traditional, except that they seemed more balanced because I had quit work to care for the baby, and with Jan to share the household work I no longer felt I was putting in a nonstop thirteen-hour day.

But as our household grew, we realized some things needed to change. With singles as well as married couples in the house, and with everyone working at least part-time, it seemed fair to share some of the daily chores. With everyone up to his elbows in dish suds and vacuuming, men found it easier to do household tasks.

We don't share all work equally in our household. Some jobs and responsibilities are assigned according to ability, interest, and available time. At one point, the women found it satisfactory to do the majority of the cooking. But at another point this became impossible because of work schedules. The seven adults in our household ended up cooking one night per week, and even guys who hadn't cooked much gradually began to enjoy that one evening of culinary creativity!

Sometimes the practice comes first and the concept later. David Moberg commented, "I agreed to cook because it was fair, but at first it was a drag. Then I realized I was serving my brothers and sisters by cooking, because it was important for the functioning of our household at this time; so I began to put myself into it with joy." (And that's the truth; all of us look forward to a "Moberg special" once each week.)

Another changing area was the care of Julian. When I was home and Dave was working full-time, it made sense for Julian's care to fall primarily to me. Living in community, however, we began to be more sensitive to the need for fathers to be integrated into that basic part of life, too. In community, it became possible for us to make a choice that affected two major areas of our lives: instead of Dave working full-time and me caring for Julian, we decided that both Dave and I would work at home and share the care of Julian. As Dave worked in the morning and cared for Julian in the afternoon, he began to realize that the quality of relationship differs between just playing with your child for an hour after supper and caring for him daily.

This realization caused us to make another change, to take turns putting Julian to bed at night. This was not only to relieve one parent from that regular nighttime duty, but also because the nighttime ritual of bath, putting on pajamas, story, kissing, and cuddling is a special time between parent and child. Both parents should have the privilege to share in it.

We've basically learned one thing about male and female roles: don't take anything for granted. If a man or woman ends up with a "traditional" role, that's fine, *if that is a conscious choice* where the needs of the individual and the group have been considered. The actual role becomes much less important than the attitude people have toward each other.

At the Society of Brothers, for instance, women seemed to have fairly traditional roles; they worked in the kitchen, laundry, canning room, the children's house. Men worked in the toy shop and the print shop, did heavy cleaning and maintenance, carpentry and mechanical chores. Some areas overlapped—teaching, administrative work, buying for the community, gardening. But even with the fairly traditional roles, we were struck by two things: first, the marvelous balance of work. When work for the day was done, it was *done* for both men and women. (The only exception was in the case of child care during meetings and visiting with guests, which were rotated among various people.) Both men and women were occasionally shifted to another area of work, and when the harvest was ready or guests were coming or the peaches needed canning, people came from their regular work to pitch in for the day. The daily work schedule allowed adults to spend time together or be alone for an hour in the middle of the day, with additional time for mothers to spend with their children. The weekly schedule was arranged so that on certain days work stopped early for families to picnic, swim, or enjoy each other in some way.

The second thing that struck us was that each person (whether preparing vegetables in the kitchen or drilling holes in wooden toys) seemed to have an attitude that what he was doing was serving the other in love. One day while I was working in the kitchen, the noon meal was ready but there was still time before the big bell would call everyone to dinner. The women and girls in the kitchen eyed the stack of pots and pans that a crew of men usually did after the meal, and decided to pitch in and do them for a surprise. By the time the bell rang, nothing was left on the sink counter except a small vase of freshly picked flowers, the crowning touch to their gift.

This way of thinking about the other person in the community—serving each other in love—

begins to affect how husbands and wives, men and women, think about each other. Am I taking her for granted? Am I using him selfishly? Are her gifts being used? Am I helping him do what God wants him to be doing? Am I doing my part as a father? And so on.

At The Bridge, for example, a three-family community in Newton, Kansas, they were working out these questions very deliberately. They decided to have two adults work at full-time paying jobs to support the community. This left four adults to work part-time or do volunteer work in various social services and projects. On the family level (each family had their own house on the same block at that time), husbands and wives shared household chores and child care and were beginning to try mutual child care between families.

While we were there, for example, Dave Janzen was using his time putting out a newsletter on prison reform and remodeling a house nearby for use as a peace center in Newton. Because of his flexible schedule, he was usually home for lunch, and while we were there he hung out the laundry or did the lunch dishes before getting back to work. Every other afternoon, while his wife Joanne did volunteer work, he cared for their two-year-old daughter Natasha and the two Schmidt children. On alternate afternoons, Steve Schmidt, another community father and a college professor in environmental science during the school year, cared for the three children.

Certainly The Bridge, being much less structured and without the history of the Society of Brothers, differed in many of the ways jobs were worked out. The three Bridge families talked freely with us about women's liberation, how to end racial, economic, and sex discrimination and about their own struggles with their changing roles. At the more reserved Society of Brothers, however, these topics just didn't come up. But in both we saw the underlying attitude of being submitted to each other because of submission to Christ.

At Church of the Redeemer in Houston, the concept of submission was given a great deal of direct attention. In conversation after conversation we heard people discuss the subject of wives being submitted to husbands, household members to the head of their household, church members to their pastor, Christians to the Holy Spirit as He worked through church leaders. This was true even though men and women shared many kinds of work and responsibilities, both in the larger church-community and in the extended households. During our visit we struggled for several days with their preoccupation with submission, authority, and leadership; gradually we realized that the basic attitude was essentially the same as in the other communities—that of needing to submit to each other because of our submission to Christ and the Holy Spirit.

The experience at Houston was hard for us, because in our marriage relationship and in our household-community we had talked freely about submitting to Christ and the Holy Spirit, but had rarely applied that word to human relationships. We'd felt that the concept of submission had been misused both by the world and by Christians to oppress people, to lord it over others, to disregard certain people (such as women) as valuable persons. But after being at Church of the Redeemer, we felt we needed to take a fresh look at what submission in the Christian sense means.

Suppose we take seriously the continual act of submitting to Christ, and give this physical reality by submitting to His Body—our brothers and sisters in Christ in the local church-community. We then realize that this also means submitting to each other as individuals. We decided to reclaim the concept of submission in our marriage: "Be subject to one another [out of reverence for] Christ. Wives, be subject to your own husbands, as to the Lord . . . . Husbands, love your wives, just as Christ also loved the church and gave Himself up for her . . ." (Ephesians 5:21-25). We gained a deeper understanding of the sacrificial love Christ intended us to have for each other.

19
Children

(NETA)

We sat over coffee in an Evanston restaurant talking about raising children in community. Across from me, Jean Howe slipped cream into her coffee as she thought about some of my questions. She had a quiet face; her long light brown hair caught back at the nape of her neck was streaked with gray.

I'd wanted to talk with Jean because she had lived in community with the Reba Place Fellowship for four years. And, in addition, she was the mother of three children—Mark, 5, and two biracial, adopted children, Kathy, 3, and James, 2. Furthermore, their family had recently moved from a single-family apartment into a large extended household.

I said, "People often ask me about children being brought up in community. They seem especially curious about the effect of the extended-family household on children—how discipline is handled, whether parental care and authority are diffused, etc. They also have broader questions such as, 'How do kids turn out who have been brought up in community? Do they accept the way of life their parents have chosen?' "

Jean smiled. "What have you been saying?"

"I have to tell them the truth—we don't have much experience in that area. Except for the first year when we lived with the Havenses, Julian has been the only child in our household. On the whole it's been positive, resulting in an outgoing, friendly little boy who gets along famously with adults. We've seldom had to get a baby-sitter for him; when we have to be away, someone in the house is almost always available to take care of him, someone he knows as intimately as a big brother or aunt. Others in our household have exposed him to personalities and gifts beyond our own, too. Dave Toht and Dave Moberg especially have brought a lot of music into our home. Becky has taught us all to folk-dance, and Julian loves it. And often an adult will cuddle up and read a story with him when both mommy and daddy have to be busy."

"Any problems?"

"One obvious one: the ratio of one child to seven adults! Julian needs peer relationships, but that would be a need even if we weren't living in community. However, one time we saw a special problem emerging. Julian was in his late twos and seemed to be regressing—talking baby talk, demanding that we sit down and play with him every minute, messing his pants. Frustrated, we sat down with our whole group and talked about it. We decided that perhaps we were all thinking of Julian as a little adult rather than a very little boy. If so, we were expecting too much of him. He seemed to be trying to tell us, 'I can't live up to that; see, I'm a baby.' We all agreed to relax some of our expectations and let him be a child. It was amazing. He seemed to straighten up in about two weeks. But out of that we realized one of our major needs was for more children, another family."

The waitress came by with the coffee pot for refills. We absently shook our heads, intent on our conversation.

"Well," I laughed, "I really don't want to talk about our experience. I want to learn from you."

Jean nodded. "O.K. Probably the best way to answer some of your questions is just to tell you what's happened in the last year. Our family used to live in one of the Reba Place houses that had one family upstairs and one downstairs. Our two families ran back and forth a lot, and we enjoyed the closeness. Then Reba formed its first ministering extended household, and the Belsers, who lived over us, moved into it. Suddenly I felt stranded. It wasn't easy to get out of the house with three little kids.

"At the time, my husband Alan had a special concern for one of the young single men here at Reba who didn't seem to be getting along too well. Alan suggested we have him eat dinner with us on a regular basis. I thought this would be a good idea, but I was also threatened. 'If Orwin comes,' I said, 'I want a woman to come too so I have someone to talk to!' So it worked out that one of the single women began coming to eat with us regularly, too.

"Hilda often came early and played with the kids while I put supper on the table. Then sometimes both she and Orwin stayed awhile after supper, reading stories to the kids and helping get them ready for bed. My whole spirit perked up.

"About this time, a number of Reba families had moved to form Plow Creek Fellowship, and for a couple of other reasons the fellowship was suddenly faced with a number of empty houses. We weren't able to afford them, so we tried to consolidate. Our family plus Orwin and Hilda ended up moving into one of the larger Reba houses as a small extended family. A few months later we became a larger ministering household.

"Our oldest son Mark is our biological child, but he'd always been insecure. To put it bluntly, he drove me ragged with his demands. But right after our move things began to improve. Orwin and Hilda, both perceptive people, would say, 'Do you notice that when Mark comes home from nursery school, he has to ask you something ten times before you answer him?' I'd say, 'He does?' I'd become adept at tuning Mark out.

"Mealtimes used to be terrible. Mark especially hassled us throughout the meal. Then we decided to have Hilda sit by Mark and pay attention directly to him. That left Alan and me freer to deal with the other children.

"As the concept of the ministering household grew here at Reba, so did our extended family. Because more people were involved, we paid a lot more attention to the structure of our household.

Mark has become a different child in the security of this structure. It doesn't all fall apart because mommy happens to be having a bad day.

"I guess mealtimes are one primary example. We'd always had a lot of company, but it had been frustrating for me to serve the meal and handle the children while Alan oversaw the conversation. Now we have one adult, other than the child's parent, sit with each child. It's my responsibility to serve the meal, and Alan's to see that there is one conversation rather than a hubbub. The children get a chance to speak too. Now table life is beautiful, absolutely beautiful."

"How about bedtimes?" I asked.

"Well, as part of our extended family now," Jean went on, "we have a mother and her six-year-old daughter living with us. Korin, the little girl, has become one of the four children; it's a brother-sister relationship. Our Kathy adores her, and they share a room as sisters, just as the two boys do.

"For awhile we thought about rotating the chance to put the children to bed among all the adults, sharing the responsibility as we did at mealtimes. But Melanie, Korin's mother, couldn't accept that. So she put Korin to bed, and we had a bedtime chart for people taking turns with the other three.

"After awhile, though, it became apparent that this was not the best arrangement, especially for Mark. He needed his mommy or daddy to put him to bed. So now I take care of the two boys, Alan helping when he can, and Melanie puts the two little girls to bed. It's working beautifully. In an extended household, we have to try different things to meet the various needs, and in a couple of weeks reevaluate to see if that's the best solution. If not, change!"

"How do the grandparents react to your extended household? Do they like having more than just their grandchildren in the home?" I asked.

"My own parents have had difficulty accepting our adopted children, James and Kathy, so it's even more difficult for them to relate to Korin. When I went to my sister's birthday party, for instance, I asked if I could bring Korin along with my three; that was fine. But if I were going to my parent's house, I would take only my three. On the other hand, Alan's mother is very accepting; I'm sure, for instance, that next Christmas she will include a little gift for Korin. We don't expect grandparents to treat other children in the household the same as their grandchildren, but we're grateful when they do."

"Tell me more about the structure of your household," I said, going back to one of Jean's earlier statements. "Why has this made such a difference in your family?" The restaurant was beginning to fill up with early lunchers, and I leaned closer over the table in order to hear.

"We have ministering households at Reba, as I mentioned before—five have developed in the last year. It's not a haphazard arrangement; each person is there after careful consideration of his needs and how they can be met. Each household has a core of leadership people plus strong supportive people plus dependent people. Because the purpose of the household is to *minister,* we must have a strong solid structure so that each new need doesn't throw everything into turmoil.

Alan, as an elder in the fellowship, functions as head of the household; other adults have different areas of authority and responsibility. Our desire, however, is to be in unity. Our household meetings operate on a spirit of consensus, where we hear everyone out and consider all needs."

Jean continued, "I'm constantly amazed. The people we live with are so wise. Not that any one of us is strong, but put us all together . . . well, each one has his strengths, and the wisdom of the strongest in any given situation diffuses to us all. The Spirit of God witnesses in each of us to what is true.

"How does this all relate to the children? Well, for one thing, we give so much more time and thought to the needs of the children than we did just as a family by ourselves. And there are more concerned adults close to the children on a daily basis to help meet those needs. Really, it's a bigger job than any two parents can handle! We've been aware of that for a long time; children need more than their parents to meet all their needs; hence, community—Christian families brought together in the unity of the Spirit to care for and support each other.

"But the households bring community much closer to the children. Before, mommy and daddy went to lot of meetings and adults did the relating. Now some of those adults and other children are in our home, so sharing, responsibility, and caring become realities for the children as well. They receive more of it, and they learn to give as well."

Jean thought for a bit. "A lot of things have changed here at Reba in the past year as the Holy Spirit has been doing a new thing. For instance, we used to be very low-key in 'evangelizing' our own children—not wanting to push God down their throats, not wanting to force our life in community on them. When someone asked, 'Do you expect your children to choose this way of life as well?' we'd say, 'Oh, no, we aren't expecting anything. Of course we'd be happy if they would, but it has to be their choice.'

"Our motives were good, but we were in a spiritually defensive position toward our children. But in the past year, we've seen that we *are* sons of God! This is an exciting way of life. So what better thing can I give my children than knowledge of Jesus? Living in community is a wonderful life, a privilege for our children. They're part of what we're all about.

"Before, the adults would share their money and possessions, and our kids would grouse because they didn't have as many material things as the other kids in their school. But the positive spirit that has been sweeping over our community lately is affecting our kids. The children, especially the teens, are realizing community is *their* adventure. They see the adults relating in their households, 'giving of themselves,' and they're realizing that this is possible only because these adults have given themselves to Jesus as Lord. None of the teen-agers are rushing into membership, but they know from the fellowship's point of view that the way is open, that their spiritual questions will be taken seriously, that the Lord wants their lives as well."

We both sat silently and let the spirit of this joy sink in deeply. Around us the clatter of dishes only dimly invaded the solitude of our booth.

"Did you get a chance to talk with any of the teen-agers themselves?" Jean asked suddenly.

"Yes, a little. I came down on the commuter train from Common Circle one afternoon and talked to Nina Belser and Mary Roddy." Nina and Mary were fifteen-year-olds who lived in one of the extended households at Reba.

They had invited me up to the bedroom they shared on the second floor of the big three-story house. Nina's dark thick hair was tied in a single braid; Mary's blonde hair was caught up in two pony tails over her ears. Both were dressed casually in jeans. We sat on the beds and just talked about community from their point of view.

"For a long time community was just routine to me," Mary said, sitting cross-legged on her bed and seeming a bit awkward about my questions. "Until last year I didn't realize what it was all about."

"I've always felt a lot of family and group security here," Nina said. Her family has lived at Reba for eight years. "The kids at school—all they have is home to go to. I have a community, a whole group of people who care about me, with activities and everything."

"Yeah," agreed Mary, "the present group of teen-agers is really developing a group feeling. We spent all last summer at the Plow Creek farm—it was exciting to do things together. And it's carried on into this year. We meet on Saturday nights and have discussions with a couple of the adults who spend time with our age group; and we have fun-times like folk dancing or camping trips."

"What about the extended households? How have you reacted to people outside your own family living in your house?" I asked.

Mary shrugged and grinned. "I don't know, it just seemed to make sense."

"Our parents relate a lot more to us kids since the household was formed," Nina said. "It's a lot more structured now, and that means the adults have to be home more of the time. We have evening times with everybody, an evening with just teen-agers and adults, and meetings for adults only."

"Are there things about the community as a whole or household life that you *don't* appreciate very much?" I asked, hoping that they wouldn't think they had to paint a rosy picture for me.

"Oh, I suppose," Mary said. "A lot of new people have been coming to Reba recently, and it's hard to get to know everybody."

"Do you think your parents go to too many meetings?" I prodded.

"They have a lot of meetings, all right," Nina agreed. "But I just accept that because it's necessary. Probably some things I wouldn't like that much in *any* way of life. But certain of them, even if they're not a lot of fun, are still important."

I was impressed by the maturity of her attitude toward the nitty-gritty of community life.

"Oh, I know one thing," Mary broke in. "When we came home from the farm this summer, the whole house was reorganized. Some new people were living here, and I really felt out of place. It was hard to adjust. But . . . well, as I've been getting more of an idea of what households are all about, I figure I just have to keep up with what's going on."

"Can you give me an idea of what your weekly schedule looks like?" I asked.

"On Monday night," Nina responded, "we have

household meeting, on Tuesday night I cook supper. Wednesday the adults have members' meeting, so I'm on the baby-sitting crew. Thursday is another household meeting. Friday the teens eat with the adults at the common meal, and the little kids have their play groups by age. On Saturday night the teens meet. Sunday morning is worship, and Sunday night I baby-sit again when the adults meet in small sharing groups."

"There's so much going on in the fellowship," Mary broke in. "I like what I see for the adults, too. I mean, three women live in this household, and each one has various responsibilites plus involvement elsewhere in the community. Nobody's stuck doing just one thing."

"I can't imagine not living in community," Nina added. "It's going to be my way of life when I become an adult."

20

Children (Continued)

(NETA)

When we were visiting Koinonia Partners, I talked to Ellen Ebersole, whose family was also visiting that week from Fairview Mennonite House in Wichita. During our conversation, the subject of disciplining children in an extended household came up.

"We talk about this a lot," Ellen admitted. Fairview was only about a year old as a community. "Basically, two of our families tend to be more authoritarian, one family much less so, and our family seems to be somewhere in the middle. In one of our household meetings, for instance, Charlotte Schmidt said she felt the other parents thought she was too lenient about snacks between meals. We've been trying to come to some agreement on snacks, because the children quickly catch on to who allows what.

"We've discussed whether all the adults should feel more responsible for all the kids, rather than each parent basically relating just to his own. But when someone else reprimands my child, I tend to feel guilty or reprimanded as well. The other parents say they struggle with these feelings too."

"How are the kids incorporated into the life of your community?" I asked.

"Jo, the seventeen-year-old, is basically considered an adult in terms of responsibilities and meetings," Ellen said. "We've been trying a number of ways to integrate the rest of the children into things. We have devotions at supper, for instance. One family is in charge of planning and leading these for a week at a time. The kids help plan and take part as well.

"After supper, two kids work with one adult doing dishes. Also, each family has an area to clean in the house on a monthly basis. Each family then decides who's going to do what to keep its assigned area of the house clean and neat that month.

"We've also begun to involve the kids in our once-weekly evening meeting—the first part, before their bedtime. This is their part, so they bring up their concerns, and they're learning to express their feelings."

Ellen turned to her son Kevin, 11, who was reading a book. "Do you feel like you're able to get your ideas and feelings heard in the community?"

"Yeah," Kevin shrugged. "At first the rest of the kids and I didn't say much in the meeting, but we're talking more now. One thing we decided is that whoever lives in a room gets to make the rules about other kids coming in and what toys they can play with."

The life of the children at the Society of Brothers gave us one of the more extraordinary impressions we took away from our visit there.

A woman had just had a new baby shortly before. She and her husband and baby had moved into a special apartment for a period of about six weeks to adjust to each other and concentrate solely on this new addition. The rest of their children were staying with another family in the community and came to visit their mother and new little brother once each day.

Snuggled in the center of the community, just a glance away from most of the other buildings, sat an attractive cottage affectionately known as the baby house. This cottage had one room especially designed for each preschool age: babies, ones, twos, threes, and fours. A picket fence surrounded the cottage, enclosing a variety of riding toys, a sturdy sandbox, and a wire coop with a mother hen and her chicks.

I was surprised to learn that after the special six weeks with just baby and daddy, the new mother would not only return to her family, but would resume her duties in the community; the baby would be cared for in the baby house during those hours.

"But what about a mother who's breastfeeding?" I asked, unwilling to believe that these simple-living people put a damper on that maternal experience.

"Most do it," was the reply. "A mother leaves

work whenever it's time for a feeding (the baby house is just a minute away). Or if the baby's having a fussy day, she may be called to come to the baby house at any time. We take into account a new mother's strength, too, and her work day is adjusted to what she's able to do. Actually that goes for any person."

Like most visitors to the Society of Brothers, I had mixed feelings about the youngest babies and children being in groups a good portion of the day. Not being "at home with mommy" seemed to go against all my cultural expectations about "what is good for little children." Yet I had to realize that the context was different. The children *were* home, because the whole community was home. And contrary to fears we've often heard expressed that communal life undermines the family, the children at the Society of Brothers seemed to have a definite sense of the family within the larger family.

I also had to admit that the mothers in the community didn't seem harried or worn out like so many mothers of young children I know who are surrounded by their youngsters twenty-four hours a day. Family life, instead of being the hectic scramble we're all so familiar with, seemed to flow in a smooth daily pattern. One day for us went like this:

We had breakfast with the family down the hall our first morning there. Besides the father, mother, and six children, the mealtime included the wife's unmarried brother and sister. After a pleasant breakfast, the father and Dave took the little children to the baby house on their way to the toy shop. The older ones held hands as they walked to join their summer activity groups. (In summer, children in grades one through eight did things in age groups.) The mother and I had another hour to do up the dishes, make beds, and get a bit of housework out of the way.

We did these chores quickly, then sat down by an open window to talk. At one point I wondered about so much group time in the life of the children. "How does any kind of individuality develop?" I asked.

"I think all you have to do is look around the homes, schoolrooms, and common rooms for evidences of the creative work of all our children," she replied softly. She was referring to the beautiful, elaborate mobiles hanging here and there, the constant flow of paintings and poems on the walls, the gay signs and posters, the colorful decorations in the dining room—especially a large three-dimensional mural set in one wall. "Much of this work is done in the groups, but it doesn't suppress the individual spirit. Even the less gifted child feels a great sense of accomplishment, a feeling of self-worth, because he is contributing to the whole. The children's work is not competitive with one production 'better' than the other. Each child is encouraged to do the best he can and is loved and appreciated for that."

We heard children calling and laughing, and we looked out the window. The three-year-old group was having a ride in the pony cart. I called Julian's name and waved to him. He waved back with a big smile, then happily jostled out of sight with the other children.

At nine o'clock I went to work in the community kitchen, helping to prepare the noon meal.

Another group of children came by on a walk with their "teacher," stopped to say hello and had a little treat. The adults and older children ate the noon meal together. Because the men did not have to begin work again until two, Dave and I had about an hour together.

At two o'clock mothers picked up their little ones at the baby house. It was Saturday, a half-workday for mothers, so along with other sets of mothers and children, I took Julian swimming in the carefully constructed swimming pond. When Dave returned from work, we fed Julian a little picnic supper, then went for a long family walk before his bedtime and the later adult common meal. (On weekdays, Julian and I played and just spent time with each other for an hour before I was due back at the kitchen at three P.M.)

We became keenly aware that although the number of hours we spent with Julian each day was less than usual for us, the quality of the time was especially rich. Julian seemed happy and eager to go to his group each day and just as happy and eager to see us when it was time for us to be together. When parents had time with their children, it wasn't constantly fragmented with cooking or other household chores or responsibilities; the time could be freely spent *with* the children.

That same night, after supper, the movie *Heidi* was shown in the dining room for all but the littlest children. It seemed like 100 percent turnout. Afterwards I overheard one of the mothers commenting, "Did you notice how tense the children were when the adults in the movie were angry and shouted at each other? They aren't used to people relating like that."

On another day we were given a complete tour of the community buildings and groups. In one large wing of the main building were the attractive schoolrooms, one for each grade up through eight. The community strongly believed in educating their own children in their early years. Their education was excellent. Besides regular classroom work such as reading, geometry, and history, the school offered art and music, pottery, woodworking and metalworking, gardening, drama and folk dancing. In the book *Children in Community,* Eberhard Arnold is quoted as saying, "One of the important obligations of education is to give equal valuation to all services and abilities, whether they are physical or mental . . . . The child will be able to develop his abilities freely only if we combat constantly and from the start the delusion that some kinds of work have a higher status attached to them than others which are just as useful and also serve the common good."

After the children finished the eighth grade in the community school, they went out to public school. During the summer, the high-school young people either found jobs outside the community to get further experience or served in one of the community work departments. They spent one day each week on an all-day trip. The week we were there the high-school group went swimming, picnicking, and hiking at a nearby lake.

I had a chance to talk a bit with one of the high-school girls as we sat together outside the kitchen one morning having a snack.

"How are the community young people accepted by your classmates in the public high school?" I asked.

"Well," she said matter-of-factly, "the kids at school think we're odd, mainly because of the way we dress. Every now and then, though, one will become a friend and will come home with us and do things with the kids here."

It bothered me that a manner of dress should become a dividing point. It seemed that the community's principles of modesty, simplicity, and noncompetitiveness could be maintained without sending their children to public school dressed in twenty-year-old styles.

One of the most common questions asked by people curious about children growing up in community is: "Do children leave home and 'do their thing' out in the world, or do they remain in the community?

The Society of Brothers is one of the few modern communities with enough years to have much experience in this area. To quote them: "During the senior year of high school the question of further training is worked out with each student and his parents. Then the community considers together, as any family would, the interests and abilities of the student in light of our limited financial resources. The young people have often won scholarships or worked to help pay for their education . . . . The wish of the community is not to hold the children home, but rather to give the uncertain every chance to be away, to see the community life at a distance, to make a free decision as to where and how they wish to give their lives." *(Children in Community,* p. 95)

We were impressed by this "time to be away" to make a personal choice. (We heard somewhere it was a two-year minimum, either working or going to college.) We were also impressed that at least eighty percent choose to return and become permanent members of the community.

We might speculate about this, of course. It's humanly tempting to wonder how much of a choice it is after living so long in a community sheltered from the ways of the world. Out in larger society, the young person may be so out of place socially that he gladly flees back to the community where he is accepted and loved.

Sharon Farmer, from Common Circle, recently visited the Society of Brothers and wrote us: "I was particularly impressed by the first-generation members—those who were pacifists in Germany after World War I. One man I met had been in jail for his pacifism, and the Society of Brothers [then newly formed in Germany] had written him a letter of encouragement and later converted him to Christianity. Such a sense of total conviction is still evident in their lives, but I don't feel it as strongly in the second-generation young adults."

Actually, it's logical that young adults who have been brought up in the community would not have the same vivid memories of the struggle of the early days of persecution. But when a young person chooses to go the way of adult membership, the choice must still be one of total commitment.

Christians like myself who have been brought up in a strong Christian home can probably identify with the awe I used to feel when I heard the testimony of a former murderer, junkie, or prostitute who had been redeemed by the love of Christ. Their passionate awareness of being brought out of darkness into light just wasn't part of my own experience. They had experienced the grace of God in a life reversal that contrasted to my own steady upbringing in the Christian faith.

The Christian life most certainly is a choice, and so is life in Christ's Body. In one sense it can never be inherited. Yet if the parents' teaching in the Scriptures has been sound, and Christ's love steadily evident, the choice may be simpler to make than for one who has to struggle with it out of a negative, alien context. Yet the commitment for both must be total.

We, and probably all the other communities we visited, have a great deal to learn from the Society of Brothers about the education and life of children in community. Not that everything is beyond question. I felt uncomfortable, for instance, about a hush-hush attitude toward sex and sexuality (although it is an understandable reaction to the sick preoccupation with sex that characterizes our society). Straightforward acceptance, education, and communication are a far healthier Christian approach in this area. But overall, it was refreshing to be around young people who had a "childlike" spirit, who had not grown old too soon.

Probably one of the biggest validations of the family-life/group-life integration for the children at the Society of Brothers came from just observing the children themselves. Even the little ones seemed happy, creatively stimulated, involved in appropriate and healthy activities for each age, and well-behaved. The whole time we were there we did not see one child crying out of anger or frustration—a common occurrence in our home and all up and down our suburban street. Neither did we see any physical or verbal fights. All the parents assured us their children were human and had the same growing-up struggles all children have, but the general atmosphere was different from any gathering of children we were used to.

As we were packing to leave, Julian said, "I want to stay here for weeks and weeks and weeks!" We knew exactly what he meant.

21

Old People

(NETA)

Our first supper at Koinonia Partners was in the tiny cottage of Will and Margaret Whitkamper. Guests for the evening crowded around the oilcloth-covered table, sat on the front steps, or balanced on the arms of overstuffed chairs. Margaret, round and friendly, served up fried chicken and homemade whole-wheat rolls. Will came in late, bewhiskered, weather-beaten, wiry, an old nondescript cap on his head. He said a polite "howdy" to all the strange people in his cottage and promptly paid healthy attention to the hot whole-wheat rolls.

Will was eighty years old, one of the few still at Koinonia who had pioneered the farming community in 1942 with Clarence Jordan. After supper he took us to see the large organic vegetable garden he lovingly tended, which provided fresh vegetables and melons for the Koinonia population. During our visit we were constantly served deep-red sliced tomatoes, okra, beets, cabbage, and turnips from the wide variety in "Will's garden," as it was affectionately called.

Work began early at Koinonia; seven-thirty found the work crews getting the day's assignments, hoping to get as much done as possible before the merciless Georgia heat began to sap their energy. But Will had already been up for several hours, leading an early morning Bible study in the tiny library off the community kitchen.

Almost deaf, even with a hearing aid, Will Whitkamper seemed quiet and reserved in his houseful of strangers that first evening of our visit. But once out in his garden showing us the carefully tended plants or sharing what the Word of God said about something, Will gave us the feeling he had all day for us. He did most of the talking, and when we had a question we had to lean close and speak loudly. Once he understood the question he always gave a seat-of-the-pants answer that made us listen with respect for his experience and wisdom. We had the secure feeling that Will was one of those persons who had arrived at a stage of life where nothing intimidated him anymore—not the clock, not who was important to talk to, not what might happen next. He was free to be himself with the person and the situation at hand.

A few weeks after our visit to Koinonia, I was folding clothes with about seven other women in the laundry room at the Society of Brothers. The table ran along one of several large picture windows. Colorful curtains ruffled at each end of the windows; pictures and cutouts by the children hung everywhere. It was a bright, cheerful room where freshly cleaned clothing, bedding, and kitchen linens were folded; some ironing was also done for large families or persons who were sick or elderly.

Among the group of women and girls who worked there were several gray-haired elderly women, sitting on stools along the table, deftly folding clothes and sorting them, chatting with each other. My ears perked up when I heard several comments in German, then someone translating—not into English, but into Spanish! I figured out that these older women were part of the Society of Brothers when they were in Paraguay, and even before that, in Germany.

Through the picture window I could see the toy factory where Dave was working. Later he told me he had noticed one man in particular, an old man with shaking hands and a slow, shuffling walk who sat at a small table each day placing screws in the proper holes in the toys ready for tightening. He worked at his own pace, stopped when he needed to, and faithfully attended to his work each day.

Again a few weeks later, we were sharing a meal with the Pulkingham household, part of the Church of the Redeemer in Houston. Some of the older children sat at a separate table, but the small ones sat with the adults at the graciously set dining-room table. Across from us, a slight, carefully groomed, elderly woman helped one of the tots prepare his plate, made sure dishes were passed, and listened attentively but silently to the conversation.

Some of the other adults teased her about all the running around she'd done that day. "You know the doctor told you to take it easy, Margaret," they admonished. "Your idea of 'take it easy' and his idea are two different things!"

"Well, there are just so many things that need to be done," Margaret said earnestly.

Later she drove us over to the church for the Wednesday night praise service and Bible study. We asked how she came to be part of the Pulkingham household.

"My children," she said, "were all grown up and scattered; I was retired . . . . There just didn't seem to be an important place for me to fill. Then I became involved with what was happening at Church of the Redeemer, and the community households seemed like God's answer for me. My children were kind of upset when I sold the house and the furniture and moved here with just my personal things. But I feel completely right about being here; life is full and meaningful in the work the Holy Spirit is doing here." In the Pulkingham household, Margaret lent a constant hand with whatever needed to be done regarding the children, the meals, and the household, besides participating in various activities at the church.

Meeting these older people brought home to us the dichotomy between society's categories and the alternatives that Christian community provides. Will and Margaret Whitkamper . . . the old shuffling man and the foreign-speaking grandmothers at the Society of Brothers . . . Margaret . . . all were surrounded by men and women, children and young people of all ages. They participated in daily work and routine of the community and also in the worship and celebrations, the singing and the laughter. They participated in making decisions (no more and no less than other committed members), had enough work to keep them busy and satisfied, but did not feel pressured to work beyond their capacity of health or skill. They knew they would be cared for even if illness or old age made it impossible for them to "put out" anymore. The elderly continued to be fully integrated into life, never obsolete, but needed and wanted for who they were.

We thought of our own two sets of parents, two thousand miles away from where we lived, rarely seeing their children or grandchildren. They weren't "old" yet; all four were still working vigorously. But that day would soon come. And in the meantime we and our child were missing the perspective and special gifts that older people could give us.

A friend of ours often brings up the concept of future security whenever we talk about Christian community. "It's fine to talk about sharing your money and throwing in your lot with a group of other people when you're young," she has said. "But suppose you throw in everything you've got, and then in twenty or thirty years the whole thing breaks up. Where will you be? You'll have nothing to fall back on in your old age."

It's understandable that she thinks it's a pretty shaky idea when she looks at Common Circle, one small household just learning what community is all about. Providing for the future of the elderly is a serious consideration. But if we believe that as Christians we should care for each other regardless of age, if we believe that the lives of the old should be integrated with the lives of younger adults and young people, then any group seriously interested in developing full community must open the way and plan for that to be possible.

What would this mean? From what we have observed, the group needs to be large enough to provide financially for the special health needs of the elderly. It also needs to provide for the many good years left after society has "retired" them. It should take special effort to integrate the gifts of the elderly into the activities, ministries, and personal life of the community.

Even a small group like Common Circle can begin now preparing not for what "might" happen, but for what we want to happen. If our desire is to develop to the point where we can care for and integrate elderly persons into community, then we can freely give our money to care for others now rather than hoarding it for our own future security. We can trust that we will in turn be provided for when we are old.

22

Benny Bargen, Come On Home

(NETA)

We don't know Benny Bargen, never really met him, although we were there the night he arrived at New Meadow Run. It was the last day of our visit. All day long we were aware of an excitement, an expectancy in the air, as people ran back and forth with blankets and sheets and other room furnishings, as children drew large welcome signs in the art room, as women in the kitchen considered how to make the evening meal special for Benny Bargen's arrival.

"What's happening?" we asked. "And who's Benny Bargen?"

Benny, it turned out, was a man about seventy who had lived a year or so with the Society of Brothers some twenty years ago, intending to join the community. But for various personal reasons Benny had decided not to join.

A young friend of Benny's happened to meet some of the people from the Society of Brothers at the February 1972 conference at Reba Place. "Have you heard about Benny?" he asked them. Benny was now an invalid, paralyzed from the waist down in a Newton, Kansas, nursing home. "And I think Benny wishes he could be with you," the young man added.

Some time after the conference several of the men from the Society of Brothers went over a thousand miles west to see Benny at the nursing home. "Benny, come be with us," they encouraged him. "We want you to come back."

And so Benny came. The Society of Brothers chartered an ambulance plane and flew to Newton and back on Tuesday, July 25, 1972. As evening approached, I found myself listening for the sound of the plane, which would land at a nearby private airport. It flew over as older children and adults rehearsed special music for Benny's "love meal" the next night. I heard people wondering to each other what they should do when he arrived that evening after his trip. Would he be too tired from the flight for them to welcome him? Would it be most loving to do nothing for the moment and wait until he had rested?

Word finally came from the airport. Benny had taken the trip well and was in fine spirits. Everyone could welcome him.

The large dinner bell rang out over the community. Two teen-age boys ran down the drive lighting torches they had prepared. Old people, single men and women, teen-agers, mothers and fathers carrying children in nightdresses all gathered at the end of the long winding drive to wait for Benny.

The station wagon (I'd seen two boys scrubbing the car inside and out that morning) drove slowly up the drive, its way lit only by the yellow, flickering torches. In perfect silence, old and young began waving. The car stopped. Two men let down the back of the station wagon and slid Benny out on his stretcher. Moved by one spirit, everyone began singing joyfully, "Welcome Home from Your Long Journey!"

In the soft light from the torches, I saw only a prone shadow in the open back of the station wagon. But I knew here was an old man, paralyzed, unable to work or contribute physically or financially to the life of the community. He had nothing to offer except himself, a brother in Christ. Benny's presence would mean constant care, a giving of time and work and cheer by many people. But because this group of Christians had totally given themselves and their resources to meet the needs and ministries of God's Kingdom, they had room for Benny—not in an institution, but in their lives.

Part 7

Some Daily Details

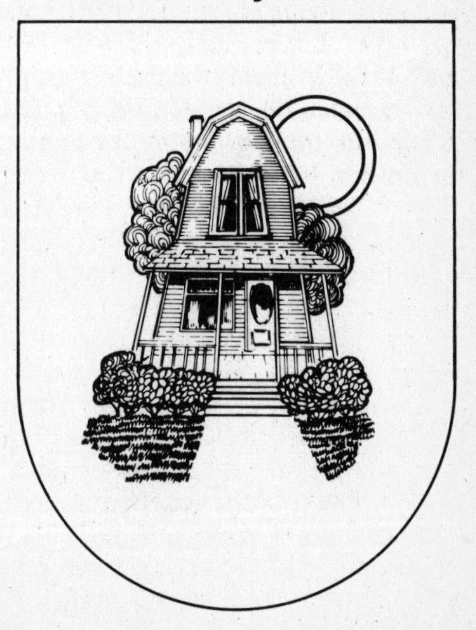

23
Extended Households

(DAVE)

The Spirit has not led all communities to form extended households—groupings of families and singles living together under the same roof. Even where this structure has been given, some members of the community may live elsewhere. The establishment of household is not a matter of principle but of need; no Bible verses command such an arrangement. However, households apparently composed of more than nuclear families were common to Paul (see the groupings he identifies in Romans 16:5-16).

Obviously, it is possible to share a common life with people who live in the next apartment or just around the corner. And it is also possible to live under the same roof with people and still shut them out of our love and life. What, then, are the reasons for establishing households? When is it useful for Christians to come together in that way?

Ministry to one another is the most important reason for establishing households. We are all far from the mature reflection of Christ. The daily accounting for ourselves that must take place among people who live together can be a good thing. In describing the reasons Reba Place Fellowship established extended households, Julius Belser, one of the elders said:

"Some of us had rich family experiences in our natural families. But many of our fellowship members were left to experience the day-to-day Christian life in an isolated context. We had a single people's apartment, but it was a pretty anemic life together. We had oodles of counseling sessions with troubled people, and in their isolated living arrangements it was hard to assist them in deeper changes of life-style. We had fatherless families needing much more support and leadership than they were getting. Now the intensity of life together is tremendous. Love for one another has some special new dimensions. The Christian family is the primary unit, and the natural family fits into that more sharply than ever before. It's an area of our lives that's hard, but also tremendously rewarding."

Church of the Redeemer in Houston first began living in extended households in spontaneous response to the need to minister better to each other and those who came to them seeking the Lord's help. A lonely older person merely wanted a family again, and someone had an extra room. A one-parent family needed help with the children.

A drug addict needed constant attention. People just couldn't send an orphan to an institution. A teen-ager in trouble with the law needed a responsible guardian, or the court would send him to a reformatory. The community's consciousness rose concerning ways to do "as unto the Lord" the little things He sent their way. In large measure this meant taking people into their homes.

Years of experience made the people at Redeemer aware of the planning that needed to go into the formation of a ministering household. They stressed the importance of adequate leadership to give power to the purpose of the household.

If it were a mutual support household where all the members were fairly mature in the Lord, leadership needed to be less pronounced. On the other hand, if dependent people were in the household, it needed strong leadership plus several support people. New Christians, children, broken families, addicts, people with various psychological problems or attitudes of hate, fear, confusion, lust, anger, laziness—these people needed the stability of strong support and guidance. The more serious the situation, the more stability and guidance was needed to support the person as he grew into healthy, godly patterns.

Graham Pulkingham, the rector of the church, recommended that emotionally disturbed people never be put into a household with children under the age of twelve.

We saw how important it was for dependent people to be aware of their role in the household. They needed to accept the support, guidance, and counsel given. (Almost all dependent people came to Redeemer in the first place because they knew they needed help.) But dependent people weren't accepted in a condescending way. They came for healing or growth, and were expected to become well and mature. The members of the household were able to maintain a proper attitude if they remembered that leadership meant *serving.* We all need each other, and we all fall short of Christ's standard.

The extended household offers other benefits, too. The Fairview Mennonite House in Wichita is a group of people who chose to live in an extended household primarily to make better use of this world's resources. Their understanding of living *in* the Kingdom of God *now* involved being good stewards of their material goods and resources. "If the world's resources are limited," they reasoned, "and some people use more than their share, others must go without. When God's Kingdom comes into its glory it would be unthinkable for the first saints in line to take more than their share, causing others to go without. Therefore we try not to do that now."

Per person, people who live in extended households actually do require fewer resources for an adequately comfortable life than people who live by themselves. They need fewer automobiles, washing machines, lawn mowers, BTUs of heat, electric lights, square feet of floor space, TVs, stereos, stoves, and refrigerators. The list is pretty long. Less consumption leads to less expense, and the option of using that time or money on more worthwhile causes.

Many American houses are empty of people

and full of wealth. This makes an almost irresistible attraction for thieves. Our house is almost always full of people and empty of wealth. It's not an important point in favor of households, but it helps provide a nonviolent deterrent to a problem that worries many people.

Some communities we visited began, like our own, as an extended household. Other communities formed extended households later as they were given that particular ministry. What is true for community in general is especially true for the extended household, where fellowship and service to each other are brought down to the gut level—our home.

24

Irritations

(DAVE)

"I could never live communally. I just couldn't have anybody else in my kitchen." We've heard it so many times.

Such a statement strikes a blow for women's lib, because it usually comes from a woman whose main meaning in life comes from housework. The kitchen is her symbolic throne, and to share it strips away identity. If this is true, more serious things are at stake than the sharing of a kitchen.

But we can make sharing easier, too. When we first started living with the Havenses, both of us left small apartments and moved into a different, large house. It was never "my" house or "your" house, but "our" house. None of us had yet arranged things in "my way" or set up household patterns that were difficult to break. I recommend that any group establishing an extended household move into a different place. But it is also possible for some people to keep their house while others join them, if that is more practical.

As new people have joined our household we have faced times of difficult adjustment. When Sharon Farmer first came from Koinonia to live with our community, for instance, she was aware of certain things we'd overlooked. Were we so intolerably hot that we needed to run an air conditioner? It was a luxury not available to poor people, she pointed out. "Considering the energy crisis," she said, "we might be more faithful to Kingdom standards by tolerating a little heat and conserving a little energy and unpolluted air."

Her challenge created tension in the rest of us. Even though there was truth to what she said, it was hard to take. Here was someone new, from "the outside," wanting to change the way we did things. If the idea had come from ourselves, we wouldn't have had to deal with our pride and stubbornness as well.

But that is exactly what flared up in us first, and when a household is being formed the members have to watch such resistant attitudes closely. When new people bring new ideas to a household, we can adjust more smoothly if we remember that we are about God's business. For instance, the person who doesn't know if she could put up with other people in "my" kitchen may find release if she thinks of it as God's kitchen. That may sound trite, but if that perspective is honestly adopted it changes the possessiveness of "the way I do things."

Three other areas create frequent and serious

irritations for the newly established household: noise, food, and cleanliness. These are points where universal standards are impossible to establish. But it will help to be willing to compromise, to avoid pressing for extremes, and to agree on expectations.

We must resist the temptation to compromise in matters of principle, but where it is personal taste or preference, compromise becomes a way of mutually laying down our lives for each other.

The person who demands the extreme of a completely dust-free, germ-free surrounding, or the person who is utterly sloppy, dirty, and slothful about cleaning responsibilities may have deeper psychological or spiritual problems to deal with.

In our household at Common Circle, we found that uncommunicated expectations were the most frequent source of irritations. It's so easy to presume that everyone else also thinks the tub should be cleaned after each use . . . that everyone knows salad and soup don't fill me up at supper . . . that everyone else wants to listen to my new record at full volume. We realized that it's important for each person to express his expectations rather than be silently resentful when others violate them.

When we know everyone's expectations, we can agree on the right course of action in fulfilling them. At times we have compromised on a middle course; sometimes we agree to do something one way one time, and another way the next. Many times it has become clear that one person's way of doing things has particular merit and should be followed regularly.

25

Working It Out

(NETA)

"But isn't it a hassle working everything out in an extended household?" people ask over and over. "I mean, how do you decide who's going to do what work? How do you schedule the use of the cars—or even the bathroom?"

When first setting up a household we face a certain amount of "hassle" as we work things out; it does take time and effort. But a lot depends on attitudes, whether a person just *has* to have things done his way, or whether a group can function as a team, knowing that everybody has to practice give-and-take. We even look on the process as a kind of game or puzzle, fitting together what we need to do with available skills, time, and energy.

When we first moved into the Common Circle house, we found that for the first few weeks our weekly household meeting was taken up with deciding how to get the work done, who was going to pay the bills, do the food shopping, the dishes. But after a few weeks, we began to get into a routine and found that we could take care of incidental decisions about the household operation, reminders of things to be done, and so forth rather quickly at the beginning of a meeting and go on to more important matters. Occasionally the household routine and who's-doing-what needs to be reconsidered, so we'll spend a little more time.

The "hassle" that everyone seems concerned about pays off in the long run with more efficient use of each person's time and energy. It also leads to agreed-upon expectations about what's going to get done and by whom. Further, it allows maximum time for other work and relationships.

Obviously, each household has to work things out for itself, just as a large family would. I'm constantly making notes of the different ways other extended households do things when we visit them, because we've found that our household benefits from an occasional change.

Here are some ways we've worked things out over the last three years—including the flaws:

When we lived with just the Havenses, things were quite simple: Jan shopped and cooked one week while I did the daily dishes; the next week we switched. Housework we did as it needed doing. Jan: "Shall we do the kitchen floor today?" Me: "Okay." One of us would wash the floor, and the other would wax. During garden-planting time, I was outside quite a bit digging and weeding, and Jan compensated by doing more of the housework. Most heavy work, including plumbing and furnace repairs and maintenance, the men did as needed by mutual understanding and suggestion, although I think we could have avoided certain irritations if Dave and Gary had made a firmer agreement about who was going to mow the lawn when and how often, for instance.

When we joined with the people who became Common Circle, we came up with a system for dishes which, though independent of rigid schedule, spread the work evenly. We prepared a chart with our seven names listed alongside several columns. A person did dishes when he had the time, putting a check by his name. No particular order was followed; anyone could do them first or wait till last; we tried merely to check off all seven names before going on to the next column. Only if you had waited to be the last one or two people would you "have" to do them.

SUPER SUDSIES!

Becky	✓	✓			
Dave T.	✓	✓			
Dale	✓				
Sharon	✓	✓			
Dave M.	✓	✓			
Neta	✓	✓			
Dave J.	✓				

This system seemed to provide the most freedom while still sharing the work evenly. Only occasionally did no one want to take his turn, forcing us to say, "All right, who's doing supper dishes tonight? Dave J., Dale, and Becky—you're all up, so decide between yourselves who gets to do them."

Housework had been a real drag, so we thought long and hard about how to make it less so. We decided that work is more pleasant if people are working together . . . ho-hum work should be made as fun as possible . . . and came up with what we called our "half-hour splurge." We decided to all handle our housecleaning of the common rooms at the same time, doing as much concentrated work as we could in a short period of time and then giving ourselves a treat afterwards. At 6:30 sharp every Saturday evening, each one of us picked a room to do (the living room, the study, the bathrooms, the kitchen floor, the halls and stairs, the dining room, and one extra job such as cleaning out the refrigerator or washing windows) and to the tune of a very loud stereo worked as hard and furiously as we could for half an hour. Then we all collapsed together in the living room to watch "All in the Family" and eat ice cream or something special. That amounted to 3½ man-hours of super-hard work and got most of the heavy cleaning. Later we extended the half-hour to about forty-five minutes, and usually somebody did a little midweek vacuuming and dusting, but it was so much better than isolated work schedules.

"You can't clean a house in half an hour!" people snorted when they heard about our splurge.

Admittedly, on certain Saturdays we had to take care of some jobs such as cleaning the basement and the porches and hauling away bottles and cans for recycling. But for general and regular cleaning, we did a passable job. And more important than a little missed dust under the radiator was the high morale.

More specialized work, such as bookkeeping, paying the bills, shopping, and household repairs were the responsibility of various people.

Cooking finally came to be equally shared rather than the responsibility of the women. In our particular situation we all had equally full schedules. We now have a set night for each person to cook (I cook every Wednesday, for example), and if a person can't cook his night, he arranges to trade with someone. Cooking only that often makes it pleasant, creative work. You'd be surprised what good meals the guys have learned to put together, and they say they enjoy it and look forward to preparing "their gift" for the rest of us.

Some areas such as yard work are still not shared adequately. Part of the reason is that we have not taken sufficient time to talk about and agree on expectations. And last year everyone agreed that we should put in the five vegetable gardens, but a couple of people did almost none of the work. We recognize some of our weaknesses and are continuing to talk about how we can interrelate different responsibilities with the time, gifts, and interests that people have.

Laetare Partners, a small community household near us in Rockford, Illinois, had a different way of working things out. Each of the six adults in the household was assigned a specific area of responsibility, some of them housekeeping jobs, some not. Their breakdown went something like this:

Rachael—Kitchen: general cleaning, floors, stove, garbage, wash towels, etc.

Dean—Groceries/cars: shop for weekly food and maintain community cars.

Kathy—Bookkeeping: handle all community monies, pay bills, keep books, disperse personal allotments, etc.

Mark—Downstairs cleaning: dining room, living room, study.

Vic—Outside: mow lawn, pull weeds, plant garden, shovel walks, etc.

Pam—Hallways/bathrooms/guestrooms: general cleaning, wash towels, etc.

Cooking—All

Dishes—All

Some extended households, like the Memphis Fellowship, arrange for one or more persons to do the majority of housekeeping and cooking for the group as their major job rather than working outside the community in any way. Even at Memphis, however, everyone took turns at dishes; other tasks, such as maintenance of cars, bookkeeping, etc., were done by other members of the group.

If we were to break it down to a few specifics about dividing up household chores and work responsibilities, here would be some to consider.

When possible, work together. A menial chore such as dishes can turn into a pleasant time of getting to know another person and sharing the events of your day. Working together on a bigger chore (housecleaning, putting up storm windows, raking leaves) gives motivation and creates a shared experience.

If possible, make it fun! So what if it sounds silly—an impromptu water fight, ice cream afterwards, jumping in the leaves, or singing at the top of your lungs never hurts and usually helps a ho-hum job.

Make sure there is a weekly meeting or a time set aside when suggestions, gripes, and decisions about work or running the household can logically come up. This could be part of a regular household meeting, a time around the table after supper one night, or whatever suits the situation best. But it should be regular so discussion doesn't have to wait for a crisis.

Agree on your expectations! Trouble is usually caused if you harbor private expectations of what you think should be happening—that other people don't know they're supposed to live up to!

Hang in there with a way of doing things long enough for people to benefit from the regularity of routine. But be open to change when and if the situation demands a new way of doing things.

Learn the difference between pickiness and legitimate resentments. Air grievances while they are still small. State your feelings; don't judge the other person's motives.

Cars

Scheduling the use of cars is not a problem limited to extended households, since any community with a common purse shares ownership of any cars. At Reba Place Fellowship, for instance, even before they developed extended households, they assigned a car to perhaps two families, and those two would work out its use. The fellowship gave priority to persons needing a car for regular use—to get to work, for instance. Everyone used public transportation if possible.

In a community or household without total economic sharing, owners of the cars generally went on using their cars without question. Anyone else wanting to use a car would ask around to see if one was available, and make arrangements to put in gas or whatever.

In some communities, one person scheduled the use of cars, and anyone needing one went to him.

The subject of sharing cars is a serious one, possibly more delicate in a community or household that does not yet have a common purse. A person who knows how much car installments and insurance payments cost, not to mention new tires and repair bills, often has a hard time sharing a car regularly with other people who think they've done their share when they "put in gas."

Like any other shared concern in community, the subject of cars needs to be talked out thoroughly.

Private and common possessions

The attitude of sharing in an extended household does not mean I can use up someone else's shampoo without asking. It's not a matter of "What's yours is mine too." An extended household may buy its shampoo and toothpaste together, and then again those items may fall under the category of personal expenditures; if so, they must be respected as such.

Children in a family are given the right to have

their own belongings which other siblings and even parents must ask permission to use. So people in an extended household have personal belongings that do not fall in the category of common possessions. In our household this includes items that a person keeps in his private room; most items kept in common rooms are meant to be used by anyone, although there are exceptions: art supplies, musical instruments, certain tools, etc.

Personal belongings can be shared, however. In our household, the females do a lot of clothes sharing. But we respect all these things as personal belongings, asking permission and returning the borrowed item when we're through. Some things, like the bikes, are used just as much by others as by the owners. Asking is usually just a courtesy to make sure no one else has planned to use them. Many times, if a person is absent, the item is borrowed anyway and reported later. Living closely together, we develop a sensitivity about the things another person feels free about sharing, and those he is more reluctant to have others use. Only rarely has the borrowing of personal belongings in our household been any problem.

26

Architecture

(DAVE)

The extended household is one place where architecture becomes important. Though many houses have more floor space than the nuclear family needs, that space may be poorly arranged for other people. Sometimes there is no choice, and in those situations the Lord's grace will be sufficient. (He sustained communities of Christians in the catacombs for years.) But where choice is possible, four things are desirable: private space, central and inviting common space, enough space, and overall pleasant space.

One has only to observe a group of people living in inadequate facilities to appreciate the work of the architect. Certain conditions incite problems. An urban studies program we were once associated with tried to house its students in an old church. What a disaster! They had plenty of space—so much open space, in fact, that people rattled around like in a pinball machine. The large classrooms in the old church were used for dorm rooms; the girls had one of the larger rooms and the fellows had a couple of the others. Apartments were devised for three married couples out of the smaller rooms. Furniture was clustered at one end of the fellowship hall for a lounge. At the other end, near the well-equipped kitchen, tables were set up to feed fifteen or twenty.

The place was functional and well-lighted with florescent tubes—okay in offices or classrooms, but stark and grotesque in a living room. Many of the rooms had no windows, and the few windows in other rooms had been frosted so Sunday school children would not be distracted by events outside. But people wanting to *live* there found their eyes imprisoned.

Christians are not to worship material things, but on the other hand, we are not to be gnostics, denying the legitimacy of one's physical life and surroundings. It is important to have some private space for each person or married couple. Our compulsion to order our immediate physical surroundings is the natural extension of our personalities. If this extension is prohibited, internal pressures increase.

In the old church building this nesting instinct became very obvious. Everyone attempted to arrange a little place for himself and a few of his things, but the opportunity was inadequate. And because the students couldn't unpack physically, they couldn't unpack mentally either. Subconsciously everyone was busy keeping himself "collected."

In time people began passing each other like

ships in a foggy night, oblivious of one another's presence, always keeping themselves gathered in. Jesus had no place to call His own, but He did need to be completely alone and undisturbed at times to meditate and pray. In today's urban maze where quiet gardens are rare, private rooms or at least some private space seems legitimate.

In our Common Circle household, the singles each have a bedroom for themselves. The married couples each have a bedroom. I see no problem with two singles or children sharing the same room provided they agree to it and the room is large enough. At any rate, a little private space is important.

So is common space in an extended household. Multiple bathrooms remove the occasion for many irritations. The common living room needs to be inviting and central so that people naturally gravitate there when they wish to relax. If it is not, they will drift off to their rooms alone. Also, children need a place to play where their legitimate spread of toys won't continually trip people and their natural noise won't interrupt conversations. The kitchen must be large enough for a couple of people to prepare regular meals for the household.

Architects consider all these things and more in planning houses. They designed many older houses for larger families, and with only slight alterations these make wonderful homes for Christian extended families. But there are diminishing returns on the rewarding life of the extended household if too many people cram into the wrong kind of space. Most Americans don't need half the space they have, but everyone needs a little of the right kind.

27

Sex in the Extended Household

(DAVE)

Bet this was one of the first chapters you turned to! If so, you're normal. Sex and drugs are some of the first images that come to mind when we hear of anything like a "commune." Some people are brave enough to ask about sex directly; others come on with questions like, "Where do you all sleep? or "Do your neighbors object?"

The publicity the media gave the hippie crash pads in the late sixties makes it easy to understand where people get their stereotypes. And because of this we take pains to avoid using the word *commune* to describe ourselves.

However, when asked about sex, we often say that as a happily married couple, we enjoy our sexual life. But we quickly add that Christian community does not involve fudging on the biblical standards for sexual conduct. God's Word is clear: intercourse is the symbol of love between *a* man and *a* woman who are united in an exclusive, lifelong commitment. Any community seriously wanting to make God's Word its standard must face this fact and abide by it.

But then some ask, "Doesn't living under one roof or in close proximity increase the temptation to sexual promiscuity?"

It need not. We must recall what Christ said about adultery: "You have heard that it was said, 'Do not commit adultery.' But now I tell you: anyone who looks at a woman and wants to possess her is guilty of committing adultery with her in his heart" (Matthew 5:27,28 TEV). Christ was clearly placing the point of sin a long time before its consummation.

When we comprehend this teaching, most of us must admit our guilt in breaking God's commandment against adultery. After all, according to Christ's standards, a person can sin as he sits primly in a church pew looking at someone who remains thoroughly concealed by a modest choir robe fifty feet away—all done in the presence of several hundred Christians on a bright Sunday morning.

When we view the sin of adultery from God's perspective, the separation of house or apartment walls cease to be very useful. The person who would please God must deal with his heart. It is not enough to place the deed beyond his ingenuity or make the social penalty greater than his courage.

Within the confines of a household or a community the earthly consequences of sin may seem more painful because the relationships and trusts broken by the sin are so much more valuable. The higher we climb, the more it hurts when we fall. God desires us to have strong relationships without falling; so He wants to change our hearts to prevent them from twisting a good thing into sin.

How do we deal with our hearts in this matter? The first step is to face Christ's teachings on the subject honestly and be willing to identify sin at its source. To ignore or compromise Christ's teachings is trouble already, and will lead to further trouble.

Once we affirm that Christ was right about lust, we must remind ourselves continually by sound teaching and wise leadership. The formation of a household should not be the haphazard gathering of a few Christian friends. Certain people need to exercise leadership. They must be sufficiently alert and strong in the faith to take the initiative in speaking up when people are headed for trouble. And as brothers and sisters, we need to recognize that we *are* each other's guardians and submit to that correction.

In the past our Common Circle household has recognized no particular leaders, and we have taken unnecessary risks in this and other areas because of it. Oh, on various occasions we've mustered up the courage to go and counsel one another on sexual attitudes and conduct. But it's so easy to let it pass and think that "it's not my business," or to pay little attention when a brother or sister does speak up.

Far from providing the opportunity for easier sexual sin, Christian community should create an environment that can help each of its members to resist the temptation to sinful thought or deed more effectively. In the scattered parish of the church on the corner, few people know enough about each other to sense when someone is confronting temptation. No one is around to give counsel when a friendship begins to take on some obviously unhealthy characteristics that will inevitably lead to trouble. But in a Christian community, and especially in an extended household, such a relationship cannot escape the attention of loving brothers and sisters. If they are committed to helping each other live lives obedient to Christ, they will speak up.

It would be impossible for anything but the quickest and most deliberately sly affair ever to go unnoticed in an extended household. Too many people are around. That is obviously not the case for most American Christians these days. It's simple for them to keep great portions of their lives hidden from their brothers and sisters. Such lack of accountability means that marriages can become complete shambles before anyone notices. It means people can quietly become lonely and vulnerable to the wrong type of relationship. It means that a courting couple lacks support and counsel for a healthy marriage.

One purpose of Christian community is to eliminate these undesirable conditions and provide the right environment for Christian maturity. In the area of sexual relations it seems important that we have a consciousness at all times of just what Christ said was sin.

Clarence Jordan, the founder of Koinonia, helped me understand and apply Christ's teaching on adultery when he wrote in *Sermon on the Mount,* "He did not say that everyone who had a sexual impulse was an adulterer at heart. That would have condemned every normal person . . . . He was saying that there is no difference between the act of adultery and the willingness to commit it" (page 49).

Jordan has touched the issue. The sin must be primarily controlled by the will. And with help from the Holy Spirit and other Christians, that is not as impossible as it may sound. For instance, most of us have had the experience of living for years in the same house with attractive persons of the opposite sex without sinning. We can live with beautiful sisters and brothers, physically mature children, or still-attractive parents without sinning because we consciously choose in our wills to refuse to see those people as sex objects. So holiness here doesn't rest on the circumstance of never seeing people in their night clothes, but on how we think of them and act toward them. We believe that it *is* possible for a person to make some conscious choices about the one to whom he will give himself sexually.

Christ taught that adultery in one's imagination was as much a sin as the deed. He did not condemn the young person anticipating a future married state. Nor did He condemn us when we recognize and appreciate someone's physical attractiveness. All of God's creation affirms that He intended physical beauty to attract and stimulate the opposite sex. Shame and guilt should never be ascribed to this natural attraction and desire; it is what you then do with the person (even in your mind) that can be sin. What Christ clearly labeled as sin was the *illicit* affair—the desire for it, imagination of it, or the act of it.

It is important to make these distinctions clear in the Christian community. A puritanical denial of sexuality twists Christ's teachings into a requirement that only abnormal people can follow. When this happens, healthy Christians are apt to be made sick with guilt; or, more likely they will ignore the teaching as something they don't know how to apply.

But there's a problem with writing about something like sexual attitudes and conduct. We all have a tendency to turn it into legalism. When we draw a line, we habitually condemn everyone on the other side, yet dance as close to it as possible without stepping over. We self-righteously enjoy our recklessness without ever considering that God may have even better things for us.

A brother challenged me to this further maturity: "It may be O.K. to appreciate the sexual attractiveness of some woman, but do you end up giving a beautiful twenty-year-old girl more or different attention than you would give to a wrinkled, seventy-year-old grandmother?" I had to admit that Christ did not show that kind of prejudice toward people.

Christ's brief word on sex did not establish a new legalism for us to flaunt or flirt with. Christ is our real Standard, our living Standard, not reducible to words. He is always calling us onward to the higher life of the Kingdom, where there is no male nor female nor marriage.

28

Beauty and Creativity in the Kingdom

(NETA)

Not long ago we received a letter from The Ark, a one-household Christian community in Springfield, Massachusetts. They had read an article Dave and I prepared for *Eternity* magazine about various Christian communities, and wrote in hope of establishing contact with others. They shared their own growth process and many of the questions they were struggling with. One concerned the quality of their physical surroundings in relationship to their belief in the simple, shared life.

They were concerned about being good stewards of this world's resources and the things God had given, but they also felt that their life and environment should echo God's ideal of beauty and grandeur. "So," they wrote, "the problem arises: do we buy no curtains and get along with only the essentials of life? Or do we buy inexpensive, aesthetically mediocre fabric? Or the best quality to reflect the highest beauty we are capable of expressing? This question plagues us on almost every major purchase over ten dollars as we try to determine God's plan for this seventy-year-old Victorian house."

The question may at first sound like an unnecessary preoccupation, since most Americans have gotten into the habit of buying the best quality we can afford without ever asking if we should. But after our trip, the question hit home. As we traveled from community to community, we realized that we were reacting to the quality of life in different ways. At the Memphis Fellowship, for instance, we appreciated the neatness and simplicity of their household, but felt uncomfortable with the general lack of music, literature, art, and the seeming disinterest in any expression of culture. The food was tasty as far as it went, but little thought was given to balanced meals; fresh vegetables, fruits, and milk were in short supply. The food question worried us, because a pregnant wife in the house was physically weak.

On the other hand, we were a bit taken back by the comparatively luxurious life of a number of the households at Church of the Redeemer in Houston. Flashy clothes, wall-to-wall carpeting, exquisite draperies, fine furniture, and expensive cars seemed out of keeping with the emphasis on the simple life that pervaded nearly all the other communities we visited.

Were our reactions just personal taste? Why

should the Christian live a simple life, one that reflects an itinerant attitude toward this world? Why should a Christian reflect all the glory of God's creation that he can? Does the community life of Christians have anything to say to the quality of life in terms of physical surroundings and cultural richness?

Living in the Kingdom

A sense of living by Kingdom values and standards began to affect our attitude toward our style of life, our material possessions, and surroundings. We had to think over Christ's admonition, "Do not lay up for yourselves treasures upon earth . . . but lay up for yourselves treasures in heaven" (Matthew 6:19,20), and "it is easier for a camel to go through the eye of a needle, than for a rich man to enter the Kingdom of God" (Matthew 19:24). We had to admit that "things" have a way of standing between ourselves and God, between ourselves and others.

During the last few years, the media have made us well aware that the earth's resources are being overused and misused by a small portion of the world's population—namely, us. Many of the Christians we've met in various communities have strengthened our conviction that this is an area where the Christian needs to give witness by limiting his own use to basic needs.

Also, most of us American Christians have grown used to a standard of living that keeps us at a distance from the poor in our cities and rural areas. In community we've come to the point of realizing that we are not possessors of our money and belongings, but stewards, charged with using them for the Kingdom, for others.

The simple life

This does not necessarily mean the drab life; it means consuming less and investing ourselves more in things of eternal consequence. It becomes an attitude of thinking in terms of needs rather than wants. We realize that this is relative. What we may consider a simple life may seem luxurious to another Christian, and it is undoubtedly extravagant in comparison to the average peasant in a Third-World country. But if we open ourselves to the attitude of wanting to consume less and be more about the Kingdom business, we will find our decisions concerning housing, clothing, food, and other things affected, too.

In one issue of *Mother Earth News,* a reader shared her formula for using resources wisely: "Use it up, make it do, make it over, or do without." Some things we can choose to do without, and our lives will suffer little for it. Alternatives? Secondhand stores and annual rummage sales have produced rugs, chairs, pots and pans, canning jars, lawn furniture, winter jackets, and toys for our household with lots of wear left—given a good scrub, a button sewed on, a dab of paint, or a new cover. As prices on food and clothing go up, we've been learning to "do it from scratch"—planting a garden, baking bread, sewing, and mending. We've tried to make a conscious effort to use only goods that can be recycled or that will decompose.

The support of the group is an important factor in living simply. After all, poor people must live that way without choice and often alone. It's an expensive struggle to be poor: higher prices for less quality in poor-area stores, high rent for miserable housing, etc. Simple living is a good discipline to spawn compassion and understanding of the poor. We've found that as we live in community, where everyone's skills, services, time, and possessions are shared, resources go a long way, and less money has to change hands. We do most of our own repairs and get by with less of almost everything per person—cars, washers and dryers, tools, utilities, etc.

Beauty and creativity: reflecting the Kingdom

Does the simple life mean sacrificing an attractive household? (I can just hear someone say, "Institutional coffee mugs? Rummage sale chairs? Ugh!")

Our visit at the Society of Brothers showed us lives and material goods that were not pretentious, elegant, or costly. Still the community seemed to burst with color, art, music, and joy. Bright colors abounded on painted walls, breezy curtains at the windows, fresh cut flowers in every room, gay signs of welcome on every door. Handcrafted mobiles hung in many family sitting rooms, and larger ones struck the eye in several of the common rooms. The dining room had a special wall mural and gay ceiling decorations to welcome parents back from an all-day vacation trip. The furniture was made out of wood in a simple but sturdy style, yet tables were covered with bright-colored, hand-embroidered tablecloths. Women and girls brought handwork to do when meals were over.

Their life was at once simple and beautiful. I thought about this in relation to the question The Ark raised in their letter. Our homes and surroundings *are* part of our witness (especially community homes which minister to visitors and guests) and should reflect the spirit of the Kingdom of God. Sinking too much money, time, or pride into our homes can easily muffle our witness and stand between us and people's needs. Yet on the other hand, drabness and lack of warmth can turn people off.

Food

If we live in the Kingdom, use resources wisely, and are responsible for each other (including our bodies), then food goes on the list of concerns for a community's quality of life. A few people have said, "Oh, come on, let's not get hung up on irrelevant things." In a sense, it's true. We realize there isn't an absolute standard about what Christians in community should eat or how they should buy or prepare it. But we decided as a household that we needed to cultivate some new attitudes: that we should be open to resourcefulness and simplicity and should pursue health.

From there it has been a process of learning by trial and error, by incorporating something new we pick up from a friend or another community, by reading up on nutrition.

Some of the things that have helped us in shopping for our particular household are: making a weekly menu and shopping list, and shopping only from the list (no impulse buying); sticking to a set weekly food budget; buying store brands or off-brand names rather than name brands (unless there's an obvious sacrifice of quality); avoiding "convenience" food (except an occasional cake mix), individually wrapped portions, fancy packaging; cutting up our own stew meat and chicken rather than paying the extra price for pre-cut packages; finding the store with the most consistent low prices and sticking to it rather than store-hopping.

We've switched to whole wheat bread almost exclusively; we've grown many of our own vegetables in the summer, have learned to sprout beans, make (and love) yogurt. We have added to our menus healthy meats such as liver and heart, and have tried to learn to cook food so as to retain the most nutrients. We've learned some healthy, low-cost shortcuts like making sour cream from cottage cheese, and we make sure we serve adequate amounts of vegetables and fruits even if it means cutting out ice cream.

Mealtime is an important communal time. There is something about gathering together at the table that we take seriously. We plan for at least one meal a day in our extended household where we set the table properly and attractively and all sit down at once to enjoy a well-prepared meal and each other's company. Mealtime is part of the quality of life of people together. It can be either haphazard or a time of sharing and fellowship. Our household usually eats breakfast and lunch in twos or threes, however it fits into each person's daily schedule. But supper brings us all together around someone's gift of service represented in the steaming dishes, and we join hands for thanksgiving and share the day's events. Several times a week we sit at the table sipping coffee or tea after the dishes have been cleared and talk on about some personal matter or something light such as a movie someone has seen. Or maybe we future-dream about an organic farm. We've found it important generally to have only one conversation going at the table at a time. With a little practice this is possible and rewarding. We've seen it work in households with as many as fifteen around the table. (One night at the Society of Brothers a single conversation was conducted among almost two hundred people in the dining room; we all ate in quietness except for the various people as they spoke back and forth. The sense of unity and oneness was electric.) In contrast you have probably been driven to indigestion at a chaotic table of six. We have.

Sometime during our evening meal Julian usually asks, "Who cooked this meal?" The person who did is supposed to raise his hand and say, "I did." Then Julian says, "You are a good cook, Dale" (or Sharon, or Dave Toht, or whoever). This little ritual he made up makes us realize that mealtime for us is not taken for granted, that all of us appreciate the time together—the cook's gift of service and the fellowship around food.

Enjoying each other

While we were at The Bridge in Newton, Kansas, members seemed to be going through a specially difficult phase in their life together. Some members were even expressing doubts about community life as a whole.

One evening we asked, "Do you have fun together?" They thought awhile, and the general response was, "Well, not very much."

We identified closely with some of their feelings because at one point in our history we had taken ourselves far too seriously. Our weekly communal meetings were usually heavy and tense, dealing with problems and decisions and relationships with no time to enjoy each other. So we took some steps to counter this. A couple of people in our group were taking a class in theater that took them through many musical exercises and games. For a while we asked them to share these with us at the beginning of our meetings to loosen us up. When things became tense, we'd sometimes stop in the middle for a little more of the same. It did us good.

It may sound strange to "make time" to enjoy each other. But if it gets left out of a group's life (or a family's life, for that matter), things can go sour. Some of the things we've done just for fun and enjoyment include occasional dress-up candlelight dinners scheduled for after Julian is in bed. Or we pack up supper and go to the beach in good weather. Or set aside Tuesday evenings to watch "Masterpiece Theater" on educational TV. Folk dancing has been an increasing group activity that we enjoy doing together. A camping trip over the weekend or a special retreat has been invaluable. On a more regular basis, members of our household have helped form a literary group which meets once every three weeks to encourage the participants in writing, photography, art, music. We often sing together, and several of us play instruments together. We have a recorder trio, for instance.

We've also found it important to develop meaningful traditions around holidays and celebrations. Birthdays are important at Common Circle, complete with decorations and a birthday cake, special birthday songs (sometimes written originally by our more accomplished musicians). Our last birthday—Dave Moberg's—we pretended we had forgotten during supper. He had to go to a night school class, and when he returned late that evening a party was all laid out on the floor of his gaily decorated room. Last Easter our household taped a dramatic reading of Dorothy Sayers' *Eleventh Play* (the crucifixion of Christ). It was good enough that a local Baptist church chose to use it for their Good Friday service.

This Christmas we're in the middle of household plans for regular Advent services and an at-home Christmas program with gifts to each other of special readings, songs, or original poems. Tomorrow morning Sharon, Becky and I are planning an early Santa Lucia-type surprise for the rest of the household, waking each person up with candles and carol-singing, cocoa, and saffron bread.

Having fun and celebrating together doesn't erase problems or bring a divided group together. But taking time to enjoy each other is an important aspect of life together, whether it's husband and wife, the family, the extended household, or a whole community. It rounds out the quality of our life together.

We didn't want the differences we felt in the quality of life in some of the communities to become judgments on our part. We asked Ed Jones at the Memphis Fellowship for his thoughts—why the seeming lack of books, records, and pictures, the seeming disinterest in the arts, literature, or "outside interests." Ed said, "The quality of life isn't dependent on these things but on good relationships . . . . Van Gogh would have been well-advised to forget his art and attend to relationships. The most important relationship is the one we have with God. People often retreat into other substitutes for quality life."

Though we didn't agree that it had to be either/or, we had to respect his answer. We also came to realize that while quite a number of the households at Church of the Redeemer seemed lavish, they were *shared* by twelve to twenty people. Where was the balance?

In general, Christ's teachings reveal clearly that the quality of our life here on earth isn't to be traced ultimately to the outward, material forms, but to the Holy Spirit.

Part 8

The Community's Money

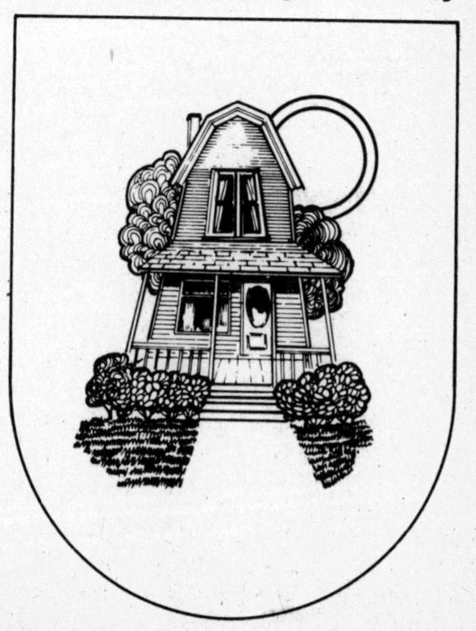

29

Why Economic Sharing?

(NETA)

Is a common purse a mandate for Christians? No. Does that end the question of sharing? No again.

We were like most Christians. We thought that our money was our business and no one else's. But we wanted to commit all we were and had to Christ, and we had grown to the place of understanding that our love for Christ needed to find literal expression toward His Body. We began to see the discrepancy in saying, "I commit myself to you, but that doesn't include my bank account or my car."

We'd been sliding along with society's perspective on possessions and money. But the more we thought about Christ's instruction about love as action, the more we realized that we needed to plunge back into the Bible for another look at how that related to our attitude toward money and possessions.

Luke recorded one of Jesus' teachings on the cost of discipleship.

"Whoever does not carry his own cross and come after Me cannot be My disciple. For which one of you, when he wants to build a tower, does not first sit down and calculate the cost, to see if he has enough to complete it? So therefore, no one of you can be My disciple who does not give up all his own possessions" (Luke 14:27,28,33).

The cross Christ spoke of is a sacrificial cross. For Him, it meant giving up His exalted place in heaven and then even His life, because He loved us. Jesus was warning us that discipleship was not a matter of lip service, but actual sacrifice. We're called to give up everything, and we'd better count the cost before committing ourselves to being His followers.

We discovered that again and again Jesus taught one attitude about money and possessions. "Do not lay up for yourselves treasures upon earth . . . but lay up for yourselves treasures in heaven . . . for where your treasure is, there will your heart be also" (Matthew 6:19-21). Christ knew us well! He knew that money and possessions tend to get between us and God, between us and obedience, between us and our brother. He was pretty explicit with His disciples: "You cannot serve both God and money" (Luke 16:13 TEV). And when the rich young man turned away after Jesus had told him that he could have riches in heaven only if he sold all that he had and gave it to the poor, Jesus said sadly, "Truly I say to you, it is hard for a rich man to enter the kingdom of heaven" (Matthew 19:23).

These passages were not new to us. Of course we'd always agreed that this was the general attitude Christians should have about money and possessions. But Jesus wasn't talking about vague attitudes of benevolence when He told the rich young man, "Go and sell all you have and give the money to the poor, and you will have riches in heaven; then come and follow me" (Matthew 19:21 TEV).

Christ was talking about action, and the rich young man wasn't an isolated case. He gave the same instructions to middle- and lower-class people as well. It was the widow's mite Jesus commended because it represented all she was. And to His disciples He said, "Sell your possessions and give to charity" (Luke 12:33). That was rather specific.

What was Jesus saying? In the context of the preceding verses He was telling them, "Do not seek what you shall eat, and what you shall drink, and do not keep worrying. For all these things the nations of the world eagerly seek"—(notice the status quo again, threatening to carry us along)—"but your Father knows that you need these things. But seek for His kingdom, and these things shall be added to you. Do not be afraid, little flock, for your Father has chosen gladly to give you the kingdom" (Luke 12:29-32).

Jesus was talking about an attitude, but one that resulted in acts of faith. And He was not asking anyone to do anything He wasn't doing, since He and the twelve disciples shared a common purse. "Though He was rich," Paul wrote, "yet for your sake He become poor, that you through His poverty might become rich" (2 Corinthians 8:9). Paul was arguing that the Jesus who had left the wealth of heaven should be our example. In the passage he was telling the Corinthian Christians to send money to the Jerusalem church, which was in financial need, "that there may be equality." Some believe their financial need was the result of persecution and the burden of feeding and housing all the new Christians who made a pilgrimage to the mother church to learn under the apostles.

In a sense the warnings Christ gave concerning money and possessions can be summed up in this: "They can easily be a stumbling block; rid yourself of them and trust Me." But there's a beautiful positive side as well. The church in Jerusalem spontaneously followed the example of Christ and His disciples and held all things in common. "And all those who had believed were together, and had all things in common; and they began selling their property and possessions and were sharing them with all, as anyone might have need .... And the congregation of those who believed were of one heart and soul; and not one of them claimed that anything belonging to him was his own; but all things were common property to them" (Acts 2:44,45; 4:32). The positive attitude was one of sharing *all* that they had with one another, an attitude which found literal expression in selling property and claiming nothing as one's own, with the result that "there was no one in the group who was in need" because "the money was distributed to each one according to his need" (Acts 4:34,35 TEV).

Paul's message to the Corinthians that was mentioned previously was not a command but his request for their expression of love to the brothers and sisters in Jerusalem. "For this is not for the ease of others and for your affliction, but by way of equality—at this present time your abundance being a supply for their want, that there may be equality; as it is written, 'He who gathered much did not have too much, and he who gathered little had no lack' " (2 Corinthians 8:13-15). (Restudying this passage was a surprise for me, because as a child I'd been taught that the Israelites who gathered little manna in the wilderness were somehow just as miraculously satisfied by a little as the people who gathered a lot. But Paul uses this passage of much and little to teach an attitude of equal sharing.)

In our individualistic approach to Christianity we had determined our own standard of living, given a portion of our net income, (say, ten percent) to "the Lord's work," and that was that. We determined our standard of living by what we could make. When we were making just a little, we made do with that. When we made more, we allowed our needs to grow proportionally without considering whether we should pass that extra money on to brothers and sisters still in need.

Paul's teaching to Timothy was to be content when the ordinary minimum of life's necessities were met. Beyond that, temptation easily set in. "What did we bring into the world? Nothing! What can we take out of the world? Nothing! So then, if we have food and clothes, that should be enough for us. But those who want to get rich fall into temptation and are caught in the trap of many foolish and harmful desires, which pull men down to ruin and destruction" (1 Timothy 6:7-9 TEV). And here the church—Christians as a Body, not as independent individuals—plays a part. Brothers in Christ who are committed to love each other, committed to live with the ordinary minimum of life's necessities, can give "all they have" to the fellowship with mutual confidence that each one's needs will be met and that the excess will be used for the needs of others in the name of Christ.

Again we must point out that the Bible does not require the specific structure of a formal common purse. But it is clear that this *was* the structure some early congregations used to fulfill the spirit of Christ's teachings. Historical records also show that a common purse characterized many church-communities even after the New Testament period. But the important point is that the spirit of sharing must find some pervasive and literal expression if we are to obey Christ. John wrote, "We know love by this, that He laid down His life for us; and we ought to lay down our lives for the brethren. But whoever has the world's goods, and beholds his brother in need and closes his heart against him, how does the love of God abide in him? Little children, let us not love with word or with tongue, but in deed and truth" (1 John 3:16-18).

Art Gish at the Philadelphia Fellowship suggested, "The minimum responsibility for any Christian in the area of finances is that he share economic secrets with his brothers and sisters." This is where many small Christian communities start: they become accountable to each other for financial needs and spending. "I'm thinking of trading in my car on a new station wagon. Is this what I should be doing?" "Mary's dental bills really killed our last paycheck, and we need some help this month." "My raise now puts my salary at $10,000." "We make an adequate salary but just can't seem to budget it. If we don't get some advice, we'll go into debt."

Once we opened our economic lives to each other at Common Circle, we began to see how we could love each other in deed and truth. Often this kind of a beginning has led communities to some form of a common purse as the simplest and most equitable form of sharing.

Economic sharing is first of all an attitude and a relationship; later comes a form, whether a common purse or some other practical arrangement designed to serve the Spirit. After a recent "shuffling" at Reba Place Fellowship, where several families moved into different living arrangements to make room for new members, Virgil Vogt commented, "The moves of the last couple of months remind me of our fundamental status here in this world as strangers and aliens. This is not our permanent home. We are part of a Kingdom that will endure forever. The occasional moves, like the common treasury, can be a useful discipline to remind us of what has lasting value."

30

All Things in Common

(NETA)

How can we work out economic sharing in community? In our own household at Common Circle, we began with sharing just the group expenses—rent, utilities, food, and other such items. We designated David Moberg as treasurer, and he opened a bank account for the group. We divided regular expenses seven ways, and each paid our share to David, who then wrote one check. We set an amount of ten dollars per adult each week for food and household supplies. In the summer when the gardens were producing we were able to cut this to seven dollars.

When extra expenses came up we'd mention them in a group meeting, and if we could swing it we'd appoint one person to make the purchase, reimbursing him later.

Because several people at Common Circle were taking further schooling, and some of us had irregular-paying work such as small-job carpentry, a home typesetting business, and free-lance writing, it wasn't uncommon for one or more of us to be at rock bottom financially when regular bills arrived. "How's it going this week, Dave and Neta?" Dave Toht might ask us during a sharing time. "Well, our check for that last assignment hasn't arrived yet, so it looks like we'll need a little help with food money," we might reply. Then someone usually said, "I've got enough to tide you over."

Our partial sharing has been a legitimate phase for our group and was an important step toward making us sensitive to each other's daily needs and their solutions. But there have been disadvantages. After shared expenses, any money left over was of course our own for personal expenses. But because of only limited income from a part-time job, Dale, for instance, never seemed to have any left over. Some had more money for recreation and casual spending than others in the same household, and this seemed awkward and unjust at times.

Another disadvantage with partial sharing came when one of us made a decision on a personal level concerning a job or use of time and then asked the group to cope with the consequences later. For instance, a number of people decided to go to school before we knew whether the group could handle it. Those involved felt they could scrape up tuition, but it left them financially drained, unable to shoulder incidental communal expenses. This put an extra undecided-upon strain on others, who either had to do without or take on a double load.

Another problem arose in the area of cars and transportation. Owners of cars retained responsibility for payments, insurance, and upkeep, plus the privilege of first claim on its use. Others borrowed a car when public transportation wasn't available. The result was that some people were quite mobile, using their car for any whim, while nonowners were restricted to "necessary" usage. It created a point of tension.

Tension also arose when nonowners handled the cars with less care than the owners thought right.

For instance, Sharon found and accepted a job which required daily transportation before she even consulted the group about whether a car would be available for her use. We finally juggled things so she could use one, and thought we'd taken a step in the direction of more equitable sharing. Sharon faithfully put in gas, but it soon became apparent that she was putting more miles on the car than anyone else while the owner was still footing a bill for car payments, repairs, and insurance that greatly exceeded mere gas. We just had not come to the place where we realized how closely personal decisions, jobs, and economics affected the group.

If we had submitted our decisions to the group and if we had had a common purse, we would have greatly eased this problem. The wisdom of the job choice could have been confirmed or questioned in the beginning. People would have had a part in accepting anything that inconvenienced them and would have recognized its value. Money from the job would have fairly gone toward the car expenses.

Let's look at how three Christian communities handled their finances:

Koinonia Partners

In its early days, when a few families made up Koinonia Farm, they held all income in a common fund, distributing it as needs arose. The families discussed all economic details together, from buying groceries to making capital investments for equipment. But in later years, when larger concerns were bearing down upon them, details concerning personal economic needs took up too much time. Clarence Jordan suggested eliminating much of the burden by shifting to a family allowance concept. Each family or individual would simply state how much cash was necessary for personal needs, and the community would provide it.

Though Koinonia Partners had become a much more complex operation at the time of our visit, the family allowance concept was still followed for the thirty-three or so partners and their families. Don Mosely explained it this way: "Personal finances aren't the whole community's business here. Rather, they're usually a matter for each family and the treasurer to consider. We take care of all housing, utility, and transportation costs in the general budget. But then each family decides how much per week it needs for food, clothing, and incidentals—usually about fifteen to twenty dollars for adults, and less for children. Then for larger, irregular expenses such as medical bills, furniture, etc., a person goes to the treasurer. If she has a question about the request, she talks it over with him. If it's a large amount of money, she consults other administrative people."

Koinonia paid no "status" salaries either for skill or tenure. Rather they made allowances based on need, expecting everyone to work his hardest and believing that everyone was equally valuable in God's eyes. All excess went into the Fund for Humanity which helped Koinonia provide employment and housing for Georgia's poor.

We asked about insurance. "We have no insurance," Al Zook, the director of Koinonia, said, "except for workmen's insurance for our employees who are not part of the voluntary community, and some auto liability required by the state. We believe God can prevent so-called disasters or use them for His glory. If He permits them, He can bring other communities or friends to our aid (something that has happened in the past), or it may be God's way of intervening in some activity."

Church of the Redeemer

Each household in the Houston community had a common purse, and designated some people as wage earners. Their paychecks supported those doing the household work or involved in the actual ministry of the household or community as a whole. No one was saving for private futures or fortunes.

Though each household was responsible for handling its own finances, all of them were interdependent and subject to the leading of the

Spirit within the community as a whole. For instance, Dave sat in on a pastor's meeting where many personal matters were prayerfully considered. One concerned a woman who was coming to the community and needed to belong to a particular household because of its ministry and nature. But since that household was full, the pastors decided to move one of its people to make room for the newcomer. But the person to be moved was a wage earner; would that create a problem? "Actually," said one of the pastors, "that household has more wage earners than it needs, so it could do with one less." The proposal was commended to everyone involved. They all agreed, and the change was made. This demonstrated to me the community's oneness, desire for equality, and rejection of personal financial ambitions.

All the households contributed to the overall expenses of the church's ministry.

Reba Place Fellowship

Members here had a common treasury for personal or group income. The fellowship then took care of all major expenses such as housing, utilities, and transportation. It met personal expenses for each family or individual on an allowance basis. Once a month it provided each family or single person a set amount based on Chicago welfare standards for food, clothing, small household supplies, and incidentals such as toiletries, gifts, and recreation. In this way everyone committed himself to a single standard of living, whether teacher, psychiatrist, carpenter, or student.

"It's true that our personal allowance is based on the Chicago welfare standard," Joanne Vogt, mother of five children, told us, "but there are so many financial fringe benefits when we live in community that it's impossible to compare it to the actual person on welfare." Joanne explained that the food allowance came to about thirty-five dollars for each adult each month, forty-two dollars for a teen-ager, less for a child. "If we have any expenses other than our regular allowance, we bring it up in our small group. When our daughter wanted to take piano lessons, we brought it up to the small group to see if it was feasible."

Irregular household expenses, such as replacement of an old couch, were also brought up in the small group. One husband told us, "We may have to wait awhile if the money isn't available, or maybe we can find a secondhand one in good condition. But eventually we meet these needs."

At the time of our visit, Reba Place had enough cars to assign at least one to every household. All car expenses were handled corporately.

The community held no personal or corporate insurance except the liability coverage required by law. Again it trusted God and His plan for His people to live in mutual support. It could then channel money into life and health and God's work rather than the country's richest business—the insurance industry.

Reba kept extensive books of its finances. At the end of the year, each family knew just how much it cost them to live, including their share of expenses covered by the fellowship fund such as housing, utilities, and travel. "The monthly allowance never seems that big," one member commented, "but at the end of the year I'm always surprised at just how much money we've gone through."

Each wage earner filled out state and federal tax forms at the end of the year, based on his actual wages. Usually all taxes had already been taken out by the employer, but if a sum was still due, the fellowship fund covered it.

This manner of pooling finances and committing themselves to a common standard of living now enables Reba Place wage earners to provide approximately one hundred forty thousand dollars for needs other than their own. Some of this money helped to support families or individuals at Reba who could not earn wages (fatherless families, invalids, etc.) The rest went to persons and projects ministering to people's needs and furthering God's Kingdom.

We were explaining economic sharing to our sister-in-law the other day in terms of what a common fund usually covered and what needs a personal allowance met. "What about a savings account?" she asked. "If I went to Reba Place, for instance, and wanted to save some money, would the community provide that amount?"

"Save for what?" I asked.

"You mean . . ." she paused, her face almost blank. "You mean people go into community intending to be there for *life?"*

I then understood a little of what she was getting at, and we talked about belonging to a Body where Christians genuinely care for each other. I explained what it meant to seek God's will together, including His will for the future of each person or family. "From what I have heard and observed at Reba Place, for instance," I said, "if a person felt that God was leading him to another place, his brothers and sisters should confirm it. If it was God's will, then in leaving he would actually be sent to join another local Body where Christians also loved and cared for each other's needs and sought God's will together. A person doesn't save money for some future eventuality when he might leave. He takes a step of faith and gives all he has to Christ and His Body. Then the Body acts in obedience by mutually caring for and meeting the needs of brothers and sisters in Christ."

Part 9

Work

31

Jobs or Community: Which Comes First?

(NETA)

In response to a magazine article we wrote about Christian community, a Christian sociology professor wrote in a letter to the editor: "Since community does not allow for the personal mobility required by modern industrial society, there is some question as to its functionality. While communities suggest permanence and might be useful for persons fixed in one locale, they might require retreat from the mainstream of contemporary life."

It was a shock to see someone claim in writing that the Christian's occupation and life-style should be dictated by the demands of a secular institution.

What did I do when I chose to follow Jesus Christ? Supposedly I left behind this world's system for the Kingdom of God and was grafted by God's Spirit into the Body of Christ. How should that have affected my priorities or decisions about jobs, where I live and how I spend my time? Admittedly, the significance of being part of the body of Christ had not been clear to me until the last few years. But when I committed myself to Christ and His Body, I committed myself to being not a "hand" alone, but a hand integrated with the foot, arm, and leg—in short with the whole body working together. The implication for me is that I can't say to the rest of the body, "I don't need you" or "You don't need me," and go off and do my own thing. (See 1 Corinthians 12:12-27.) When I speak of *Christian* community, believers gathered to seek God's will together, I can't say, "Well, I question its functionality, since that kind of commitment doesn't allow for the personal mobility required by modern industry."

While visiting the Fellowship of Hope, a small but growing church-community in Elkhart, Indiana, I learned that one couple had left the fellowship "over the job question." The husband was a teacher, and the right kind of job just didn't turn up in Elkhart or the surrounding area. He felt his job took priority over his relationship to the fellowship and left for Texas when he was offered a promising position in his field. It was clear that the group felt badly about the choice, because what had happened was against consensus. (Nevertheless they had accepted it, given the couple as much help as they could, and still maintained regular correspondence.)

The Fellowship of Hope struggled with this

matter again when Keith Kingsley was offered a professorship at nearby Goshen College. The question was not distance, but where Keith should channel his energies. He told us that after a painful process, he decided to turn down the job offer because it would have drained his energies and resources from the fellowship, which desperately needed them at that time. (At the time of our visit, the community was supporting Keith and his family so that he could take on responsibilities among them full-time. It was a source of strength to the community to have someone available at all times to meet the needs of visitors as well.)

In my own background and church experience, it was taken for granted that while you were in a certain place, you found a church where you worshiped. But if your company wanted to transfer you to another city or state, or if opportunities opened up elsewhere, you left and looked up another church when you arrived in the new place. Jobs touched people's lives every day; church life, the fellowship of believers, did not. Also, I got the impression that the "gifts" given to Christians by the Spirit were closely equated to skills. So it was natural for individuals to pursue their various job opportunities, and the church, as a body of believers, didn't have much to do with it.

Somewhere in the process of experiencing and learning about church-community, three things made me reconsider all that:

First, life-directing decisions (concerning my job, for instance) do affect the Body of Christ, and therefore should take place within the Body. Second, living in the Kingdom of God changes many of the considerations on which I might make many job decisions. Third, spiritual gifts given each of us by the Holy Spirit are for the purpose of building up the Body and may have little or nothing to do with our occupational skills or training.

The task of Christians gathered in community is to seek God's will, both for the Body as a whole and for the people within it. If I am unwilling to trust God's people with this area of my life, then I must ask myself whether I am not also holding back this area from God. If I make a decision concerning my occupation or a particular job that cannot be confirmed by my brothers and sisters in Christ, then I must seriously ask myself whether this is God's will for me.

The emphasis in Christian community of living in the Kingdom of God right now and ordering my life by Kingdom values has also changed the basis on which I make a decision about a particular job. Here are three factors that now carry less weight:

"It would mean more status and a promising future." Yet Scripture tells me to beware of wanting people to look up to me. My attitude as a Christian should be that of a servant.

"It would mean more money." Money is a crucial factor even in community decisions; we can't seem to live without it in our society. But it has become an all too commonly accepted concept even among Christians that if you have a chance to make more money, you automatically do it. Suppose that I want to make more money merely to raise my private standard of living. Especially if this keeps me from community, it is contrary to the spirit of sharing and sacrifice which is supposed to characterize Christ's Body. In a real sense, making more money becomes an irrelevant personal goal when I commit myself to a common standard of living with my brothers and sisters in community, where each receives what he needs regardless of how much or how little he happens to make. The apostle Paul said that "if we have food and clothes, that should be enough for us" (1 Timothy 6:8 TEV).

"It would mean more security for my family." As a parent and wage earner, I have to consider security for my family. But in community where my brothers and sisters are committed to me and my family, including our finances, security is a shared burden and can take second place to other work of the Kingdom. God has promised that if His Kingdom is put first, He will see to these other necessities.

My job came to have less significance for me when I realized that God " 'gave gifts to men' . . . for the equipping of the saints for the work of service, to the building up of the body of Christ" (Ephesians 4:8,11,12). In other words, the purpose of the gifts God gives us is directly related to the Body of believers—to build it up, to prepare it for service, to bring it to maturity. The whole weight of the New Testament teaching on gifts is directed not to an individual becoming a successful businessman, or getting in a top salary range, or becoming known as a brilliant artist, but to building up a Body of people that will glorify Jesus Christ. This is the primary purpose of the Christian life and must be the context in which I make decisions concerning my job and occupation.

As I studied the various New Testament passages concerning the gifts the Holy Spirit gives each child of God, I realized that they may have nothing to do with occupational skills and training. The apostle Paul, for instance, had the gifts of apostleship and teaching, rather unrelated to his skills as a tentmaker. It was a major revelation to me that my spiritual gifts may be something quite different from some ability I developed on my own.

Of course, any abilities I have are gifts from God and any use of them must honor the Giver. But all men are given this kind of gift. Spiritual gifts, however, are given to the believer to build up the Body of Christ. And I believe that discovering and using my spiritual gifts "for the common good" (1 Corinthians 12:7) within the Body of Christ must take priority. How sad it would have been if Paul had put tentmaking first. In other words, decisions concerning my occupation or use of any other talent must take place in the context of how God wants me to exercise my spiritual gifts hand in hand with those of other members of His Body.

The reason this was so new to me was that only as I began experiencing community did I begin to have any sort of *Body consciousness*—the overwhelming implications of what it means to be part of the Body of Christ. I have had to realize that where I live and what I do with my time affects the local Body of Christ, because these factors affect how and with whom I exercise my spiritual gifts (or whether I am ever able to discover what they are). In the past I have allowed job considerations to dictate where I live and what I do with my time. That's not the way it should have been, even though my particular skills as a writer and editor were being used to further the work of Christian organizations. Those organizations did not operate as a local church or Body, and that is what every Christian should be subject to. I don't mean to assume that the Christian must automatically face a conflict between his job and Christian community, of course. Also, I don't want to sound too simplistic about the complex decisions concerning jobs. Each situation is different, and the community must give prayerful consideration to the questions that arise.

We must choose between two views: will Christians allow the demands of a job to keep them from committing themselves to each other and to God's work first? Or will they seek His mind concerning their work with brothers in Christ in the context of the needs and ministries of the church-community?

I believe the latter.

All Christians should be in *full-time* Christian service to a specific Body—not just a few called "clergy." Whether our role is to maintain an orderly household, provide financial support for the community, or be a teacher or evangelist, we should perform every duty for Christ as His Body among us.

32

The Nature of Work

(DAVE)

Some Christians believe we should avoid certain occupations. I used to think this was pretty narrow-minded. If we could somehow sprinkle Christians through all levels of business, politics, the military, etc., other people in those professions would be inspired to higher moral conduct, and the world would be the better for it, I thought.

But this by-passes any critical challenge to the nature of a job.

My Christian school and church thought highly of young people preparing for "full-time Christian service" (meaning a career with a Christian organization), but also specially respected "successful" Christian businessmen, converted movie stars or entertainers, religious war-heroes, and most of all, Christians successful in professional sports.

But what about the person in a unglamorous servant role? Or the businessman who failed because he refused to make deals that would help him at the expense of others? Aren't those people our more Christlike models?

After college I became rather disillusioned with the I-can-pursue-any-career-and-still-be-a-Christian attitude. It left too many doors open to creeping materialism, blind militarism, pragmatic politics, and self-serving interests. Few Christians had career values much different from John Q. Average American. If you were technically "honest," you'd done all that mattered. So once a man decided to train for a certain occupation or take a particular job, it was easy to "do what's necessary" to succeed in that job without asking any questions. Rocking the boat became pretty risky, because a lot of training and/or seniority might go down the drain.

The whole specter of recently exposed corruption in government is a sad example of ethics compromised in order to succeed in a job. It's the do-what's-necessary syndrome; the end justifies the means.

The nature of work arises in community for two reasons. A Body consciousness inspires people to be more aware of what they are doing with their time. And also in a community where believers are accountable to one another, a person's actual practice is not hidden.

It would be a mistake to create a list of occupations unsuitable for Christians. Such pigeonholing is futile, because as society changes, formerly acceptable tasks are warped and others become harmless. Satan is always shifting his tactics, and only a few things have historically always hurt people.

The main question is whether a Christian is free to operate in a genuinely Christlike manner toward an end that will please God. This includes never having to put on a false front to impress anyone. To follow Christ, Zacchaeus the tax collector realized that he had to make a total change in his way of operating. Given the nature of tax collecting in that day, we could speculate that he would have gone broke implementing his new standards. It therefore may have become clear that tax collecting was not a viable occupation for the Christian of that day. But the point is that when Zacchaeus accepted the new standards, Christ said, "Today salvation has come to this house" (Luke 19:9).

The Bible presents some general standards by which to measure one's work. Any activity that conflicts with the nature of the Kingdom of God when it comes in its fullness should be shunned by a Christian now. We previously mentioned Jeff Wright at the Philadelphia Fellowship. His occupation as a physicist developing a laser beam weapon for a munitions company was an example of a job that the Spirit revealed to be inconsistent with the Kingdom. He quit on faith even before he had found another job in physics.

Paul briefly touches on other general standards for evaluating work in his letter to Titus. "Those who have come to believe in God should see that they engage in honorable occupations, which are not only honorable in themselves, but also useful to their fellow men . . . . And our own people must be taught to engage in honest employment to produce the necessities of life; they must not be unproductive; (Titus 3:8,14 New English Bible). Paul brings out two things here, the nature of the work itself and the purpose for which it is being done. Certain words stand out: *honorable . . . useful . . . honest . . . necessities of life . . . not be unproductive.*

Several communities we visited were struggling with the points in this passage. One member at Koinonia questioned whether Koinonia should be producing such "luxury items" as fancy pecans, chocolates, and fruit cakes. They did provide employment for local people and their profits helped build low-cost housing for the rural poor. Did that redeem them by making them "useful"?

Other questions we came across: What about speculation in such things as stocks or real estate? If a person's profits often come at someone else's loss, are they dishonorable? How about pyramid companies like Amway in which the people at the top so distinctly benefit from the profits earned by the work of other people? Is that "honest"?

At Common Circle we've talked long hours about the place of the arts in the life of the Christian Body. Music and art may not seem like the "necessities of life" or "useful" occupations at first glance, but how poor and unheavenly our lives would be without the music we sing and play, the paintings and handcrafts that capture and share our thoughts and feelings and reflect God's love and majesty.

We can't easily solve such questions, but we should consider them prayerfully.

After we have measured a job by the ethics of the Kingdom and evaluated it in terms of the advice Paul wrote Titus, we can test the nature of an occupation a third way: does it serve others? Any job can be said to serve others if the money it earns is given to others, of course. But work that is "exciting" or "important" in itself without rendering a service is of little value for the Christian. The polite question between new acquaintances is usually, "And what do you do?" The average person is somewhat chagrined if he cannot respond with some glamorous title. Instead of romanticizing the "successful" business or professional person who reaps great financial and personal rewards, Christian culture should hold in high esteem the jobs and occupations, whatever they might be, which truly serve. "You're a janitor at a hospital? I thank God for you!" Diligence and top-quality work are important in the work of a Christian but should not result from an ambition for advancement and position. Christ taught lowliness when He washed the disciples' feet, and He emphasized that "if any man wants to be first, he shall be last of all, and servant of all" (Mark 9:35). Positions with prestige have their reward now, but in serving others we render worship to God and will receive a much more valuable reward in the Kingdom.

At Common Circle we showed appreciation for service by recognizing its importance in simple household tasks before we applied the "service" principle to outside employment. Cooking was a necessity that seemed mundane. We all took a turn one night a week because that seemed wisest for our schedules. But no one particularly enjoyed it until, as Dave Moberg pointed out to us, "I began to realize that when I cooked the Thursday night meal I was *serving* all the rest of you. Then the job took on new joy, and I began putting myself into it as a gift to you."

Paul wrote, "Let love make you serve one another" (Galatians 5:13 *TEV)*. So often food for our egos motivates us to do something. But like money or possessions, our egos often separate us from other people and God. Prestigious jobs that primarily feed our egos thereby become nearly as dangerous as wealth to the person who wants to enter the Kingdom of God. We must perform that kind of job with great caution, or we will be tempted to find our fulfillment in the job rather than Christ and His Kingdom.

Secular society believes that quality work demands some kind of personal motivation; it usually offers prestige and/or money. The Christian is inspired by the pleasure of our Lord. We await His "Well done, thou good and faithful servant." Unfortunately, that is a pie-in-the-sky promise for the average Christian who is uninvolved in a local Body of Christ where His presence is made real and His authority can, to a degree, express such validation even now. But for the believer in church-community it is a powerful and effective motivation. We want to please Christ more than anything else.

That may sound utopian, but it's real. Once Russ Harris, a friend from Reba Place Fellowship, and we were speaking to a group of educators. One man in the audience, curious about Reba's common purse and rather basic standard of living, asked Russ, "If your members receive only a basic monthly amount for their needs regardless of how much their actual salary is, do you find you have some members who sluff off at their jobs, don't work hard for a raise, do just average work because there's no motivation?" I was tempted to smile, but I appreciated Russ's serious answer. "No," he said, "I don't know that we've ever had that kind of a problem. But if we did, we'd confront it on a spiritual level. For one thing, our basic motivation for any kind of work—our jobs, work in the community, in our homes—comes from a sense of serving one another. Some of our work results in a paycheck, but this has little to do with our motivation, except that paychecks do meet the needs of our families and the ministry of the community as a whole. We are called to do the best job we can, whether it's serving each other within the community, or the persons we work with in our jobs."

A woman in the audience spoke up. "I don't know about everyone from Reba Place, but one of their members is a fellow teacher of mine, and I can verify that she happens to be one of the best teachers we have."

33

Common Work or Outside Jobs?

(NETA)

I was fascinated when I first met people from the Society of Brothers and learned that none of their members worked in outside jobs. Their people were either involved in the daily life-support responsibilities of the community (food preparation, child care, education, management, maintenance, etc.) or they worked in the common industry workshop, building toys. Up to that point I had assumed that unless you lived on a farm, even community people would have to work at individual outside jobs.

Koinonia was another example of common work with their partnership farming, low-cost housing, sewing industry, crafts, mail-order pecans, candies, and fruit cakes.

I knew that communities of the past or rural

communities had to create their own livelihood, but for some reason I had just assumed that the newer communities with their access to the general job market would take advantage of it.

But my assumptions were wrong. Some communities have chosen forms of common work for specific reasons. For Koinonia, everyone was involved in the common work of the community because that *was* the community; their work had become the ministry or purpose for which Koinonia existed. At the Society of Brothers, on the other hand, the work existed *for* the people who had been gathered together for reasons they felt were more fundamental. A common work was just one extension of the total life of a common people.

Common work, we've discovered, has become an option chosen not so much for survival as for other benefits it offers.

The Society of Brothers felt strongly about common work. Working together to support themselves allowed them freedom from the crushing pressures and impersonal demands of the business world and job market, which are driving many of the rest of us crazy. For them, common work was a disciplinary environment in which personal competitiveness has been removed and the related ego problems could be dealt with. The person who had been destroyed because he couldn't measure up to some earthly standard was able to find his fulfillment simply as a servant in the new Kingdom. Also, the person who had found his meaning in terms of his accomplishments could strip away such temporal ego trips and learn that the only lasting investment of his life was in service to Christ and His Body.

This was not seen as a one-time rehabilitation effort. The Society of Brothers seemed to see the dog-eat-dog life of this world's system as universally undesirable. They believed that part of God's new order consisted of proper attitudes toward work, fostered in a permanent, healthy work environment.

With a common work, even the old, unskilled, or handicapped person contributed to the life of the whole. Working together in the routine of daily life allowed the members of the community to serve each other practically on the most basic level. We noticed that this group of people, who not only lived together but worked together, had an unfragmented fellowship that permeated the whole of their life.

The possibility of a common work intrigued our household at Common Circle. So often we experienced frustration because the pressures and demands of our various jobs left all too little time to meet each other's needs adequately. Dale, for instance, held two part-time jobs, one in the early morning and one in late evening. This clashed so regularly with everyone else's schedules that we had difficulty planning Bible studies or activities the whole group could take part in.

We also realized that our energy, channeled into so many different jobs, was rather dissipated. If we could put some of this energy into the same work, we might be able to accomplish far more in less time. A group work would also open up possibilities for ministry because of a flexible schedule. This seemed rather remote as long as each of us was involved in a different job.

We tossed a lot of questions around. Would we become saturated with each other if we not only lived together but worked together? Would this arrangement turn us inward as a group? What were the possibilities for a common work with such a small group as ours? Were we in danger of tying into something that would end up sapping all our strength just to make it go?

Reba Place Fellowship was a community that urged its members to hold jobs outside the community as a means of daily contact, ministry, and witness in the world. Many Reba people were in the social or psychological services, education, and so forth. But Reba also represented a wide spectrum of jobs, from computer programmers to carpenters to secretaries. Wages from these jobs and occupations helped support the overall ministry of the community, including the special ministry to broken families, troubled persons, and the ill.

Yet gradually, Reba, in response to needs both inside and outside the community, developed several community ministries which involved a number of Reba people in common work. One of these was a nursery school staffed by Reba women and men. It was attended not only by fellowship children, but also by those of the neighborhood. Two of the most recent developments included a silkscreening workshop and a work crew to remodel and maintain fellowship buildings and do outside contracted jobs.

A main purpose of these last two common-work projects, one member said, was to integrate long-term visitors into the life of the community. Common work provided meaningful activity alongside fellowship members; this also helped pay for their stay in the community. "We can't tell someone to go out and get a job for two weeks. But we can feel comfortable about sending him over to the workshop after we've become well-acquainted and have shown him around. There he can continue to relate to fellowship members and get much more of the flavor of life around here. Often a work situation also brings a number of spiritual problems into focus—pride, rebellion, anger. If a person has come to the community for healing and is open to our counsel, working together gives us a lot to go on."

For certain members of the fellowship, the common work was also meeting needs that couldn't have been met in the regular job market: a member who needed flexible working hours because of other community or family responsibilities, a person with severe psychological problems who needed the special care of Christian co-workers, a person going through a difficult growth struggle in his marriage who needed to be out from under the pressures of his former job for an indefinite time.

Reba Place experienced some birth pangs in these new ventures into common work. The distribution of the silkscreened prints was not going too well, and the community was seeking another project that could pay its way. However it was becoming convinced that common work played a part in the life of their community, and it was willing to give this new direction the continued prayer and effort it needed to develop.

Reba also found value in another arrangement: teams of people working together for outside employers. At one time more than half a dozen were working for the same department in the Chicago State Mental Hospital. People from psychiatrists to aides worked as an effective team that pleased the hospital. Also, a local contractor hired an all-fellowship crew to do his siding work. He appreciated the quality of their work and didn't mind some personnel changes just as long as there were enough men to get the work done. A landscaper subcontracted a whole portion of his business to a fellowship crew because of their trustworthy reputation.

It was helpful to us to witness a community such as Reba which started out where we are now (with everyone working at individual jobs outside the community), and then developed some forms of common work. As life and ministry became more and more integrated in community, common work (for at least part of the community) played a significant role in building community life and meeting both community and individual needs.

Part 10

The Community's Goals

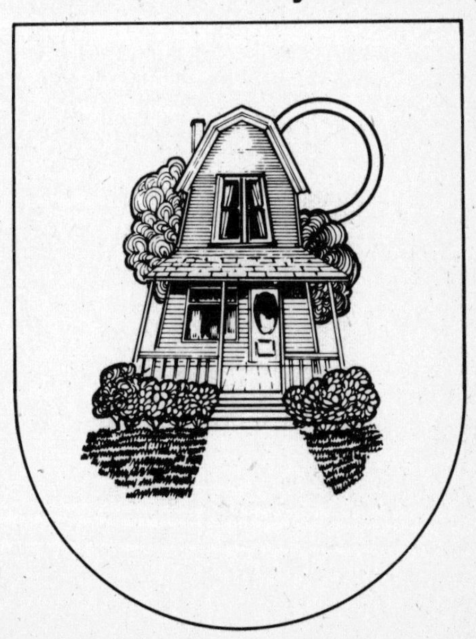

34

Community: A Means or an End?

(NETA)

"I'm against community for the sake of community!" Bill said emphatically. "It will turn in on itself."

We were talking together with several members of the 507 Atlanta Avenue community about the purpose and meaning of community life. "We don't presuppose that this particular group has any future," Bill continued. "Our way of life here at this time is only a means to enable us to reach out in a radical way to the people around us."

I was puzzled by the phrase that kept cropping up: "community for its own sake." It rang a bell with some conversations we had when we were at Koinonia Partners a few days earlier. We'd been sharing supper with Jim and Kit Gauss and their lively children when Jim had said, "Most

Koinonians feel that community is only a means to implement the primary aim of outreach—building low-cost housing, providing employment for the local poor, being involved. But I have to admit I'm frustrated. A lot of times relationships go undeveloped and a lot of our own needs for fellowship and support aren't met. Time and energy go first into the service industries and only second into community. I'm beginning to feel strongly that community must have priority over business and service matters."

I thought a lot about whether community was an end or merely a means. If the people who insisted that they weren't interested in "community for its own sake" were afraid of becoming ingrown and exclusive, their reaction was perhaps understandable.

But something was wrong. My understanding of community was that *community is relationships.* And relationships can never be used as a means, only as an end. It's the same with marriage. I didn't marry Dave as a means to some other end. Our marriage is a primary relationship in itself. One of the results of our love for each other is the huge responsibility we share for our child. But we didn't have children to justify our relationship with each other. Marriage is an important primary relationship in and of itself, and deserves basic time and effort to develop a supportive relationship "for its own sake."

However, having a strong primary marriage relationship has not excluded other relationships, activities, responsibilities, concerns. In fact, it's strengthened our ability to relate to others and take on certain responsibilities.

The Christian community is a primary relationship. When we accept the commands of Christ in our lives, we also accept a relationship with Christ's Body here on earth. We accept our fellow Christians as brothers and are united to live together doing Christ's work here on earth. This *life together* means Christians gathered into communities (whatever the form) where our lives and all that we have is shared, and we mutually love and support one another in the ministry Christ gives us.

As I tried to share this, a visitor at 507 said, "Well, that doesn't sound like community for community's sake if it recognizes its responsibility to the world and its neighbors."

No, I explained, it doesn't. But the distinction becomes clear when a choice of priorities has to be made. For instance, Koinonia was obviously swamped with visitors. Everyone seemed exhausted. Jim Gauss said, "I hardly even try to relate to visitors any more. We have so many we don't even have time to relate to each other."

My question was: is community valid enough "for its own sake" to lay other things aside, to be strengthened, to make decisions, to build up the primary relationships so that in turn the people within the community may be strong enough to reach out again to others?

At Plow Creek Fellowship, Reba's sister community, one of the members said to me, "Being must come before doing. Ministry is an outgrowth of *being* a Body. When we minister effectively within the community to each other, outgrowth is inevitable, and we should be wide open to it."

In line with this question of whether community must be formed around some outreach to justify its existence, I came across an article in an April 1972 *Faith at Work* magazine entitled, "The Church Does *Not* Exist for Mission." The author told about a church in Kansas City which meets, not to evangelize or do a task or get involved in social action, but to "be the church." "If we can really learn to love Jesus and love each other," the pastor was quoted as saying, "everything else that is supposed to happen will happen." What about evangelism? the writer asked. The pastor replied, "Ninety-nine percent of the admonitions [in the New Testament] are about how to love each other. And I think if we learn to do that right, the world will be knocking on our door. People want in on love." It was obvious in the description of the church that people were flocking to the doors, "so much so that the fellowship is having to wrestle with what to do with the demand." Another member responded to this by saying, "I've finally had to face the fact that people don't save the world; God does. But if we really love each other, we give the Holy Spirit a handle with which to [work] . . . . Any time evangelism succeeds, it is because *fellowship* has taken place. Nothing much will happen without it."

While visiting Church of the Redeemer in Houston, I noticed a brochure announcing a Weekend of Renewal which had listed as one of the topics, "Ministry: the Christian's Primary Commitment." I asked someone what this meant, wondering if we were back to the old community-as-a-means-or-an-end question.

"One thing for sure," was the reply, "community isn't a bunch of people getting together for fun and games! We are together for a purpose—to minister to one another. Love isn't easy. It demands time, energy, total commitment."

There was the key to the paradox. Community begins with ministry to each other. The result of this primary focus became apparent as another Redeemer member explained to us how the Lord spent about four years "building up the Body in real community life." "We didn't have much outreach those first few years," she explained, "because the Holy Spirit was preparing us, teaching us what it meant to lay down our lives for each other. Then one day it was as if the 'walls' that were around us were taken down and people started pouring into the community, coming for help, healing, renewal. Ministry? It's an outgrowth of our life together. When we commit ourselves to each other we commit ourselves to ministry."

At Common Circle, during a time when we were discussing possible outreach to needs around us in our town, and ways we should respond to events splashed across the headlines, we were also going through a fragmented and irritable time with each other. I was jolted by the thought, "If we can't love each other as brothers and sisters in Christ, we have no business thinking we can love other people outside the Body."

If we ignore or subordinate ministry to each other within the community, our outreach will be powerless.

35

Power for Ministry

(DAVE)

Up until 1971 life at Reba Place Fellowship might have been characterized as a plodding discipleship without much power for ministry or joy in worship. Then they were challenged by people involved in the charismatic renewal to rethink the intended role of the Holy Spirit in the life of the church-community. Jesus had promised to send the Holy Spirit, not only to comfort us with His presence, but to give us power to minister. "You shall receive power when the Holy Spirit has come upon you; and you shall be My witnesses" (Acts 1:8).

Reba people asked themselves what this meant. Certainly He dwelt in the hearts of all true believers, but what was His function in the corporate life of the church? And what did a baptism with power mean? The New Testament told of groups opening themselves to the Holy Spirit in a unique way and experiencing dramatic things as a result. After a time of study and prayer on the question, the members of the fellowship opened themselves individually and corporately to whatever the Lord had in store for them.

Since that time the size of Reba Place more than tripled. People began coming as fast as they could receive them. They formed several ministering households and recognized the elders the Lord was raising up among them. Dramatic breakthroughs and even miracles occurred in the spiritual growth and healing of many people. There came a new awareness of God's leading and a willingness to follow.

One member put it this way, "Now when a seeking person asks about the Good News, we share with him the fullness of God's plan: forgiveness of sin by faith in Christ, the sacrament of baptism in water to show his new position as a son of God, membership in a local Body designed for support and growth, and the baptism of power and joy available from the Holy Spirit. Why withhold any of the resources of the Kingdom from the person who really wants to follow Jesus?"

Before we left on our trip we knew something had been going on at Reba Place. We were aware of the external changes and could see things had really started to move, but we did not learn of the details until we returned from our trip and started asking questions. Our questions were inspired by other encounters with "Spirit-filled" communities on our trip.

During my Christian life I had previously dismissed any charismatic influence because most Pentecostals I knew fit into negative categories. They usually did not comply with Paul's I Corinthians 14 teachings on the orderly exercise of such things as tongues. Their lives frequently reflected an emotional and spiritual instability. I used these two generalizations to justify the dispensational teaching that the baptism of the Spirit was not valid in modern times.

Then we visited Church of the Redeemer in Houston!

My stereotypes were smashed. Never had I seen such order in worship blended with such freedom. I Corinthians 14 was followed precisely; there was no chaos or confusion. People's lives were stable and growing. Troubled people who came to them were calmed and established on the solid rock of Christ. Tongues were common in private prayer, as an interpreted prophecy, or during singing in the Spirit. But they were not flaunted. Other gifts of the Spirit were clearly recognized as more useful.

And I guess it was the exercise of some of these other gifts that influenced me most. In counseling sessions I observed people exercising the gifts of discernment and knowledge. They accurately knew facts about people and their situation that they had no natural way of knowing. Teaching was different from the shotgun approach I was used to. It always addressed the specific needs of the hearers in a clear and direct way. I met a woman who had been healed of massive bone cancer, and she had before-and-after X-rays to prove it.

Most important, none of these things were a

fetish in themselves, nor were any people receiving glory or recognition for them. Everything pointed to Jesus Christ, and I observed that the practical results of this community's life and ministry was to bring people to Christ.

The only thing Neta and I could do was go back to our Bibles to recheck all those dispensational dismissals we had accepted.

Five events said much to us about the filling of the Holy Spirit: (a) the Spirit-baptism of Jesus which launched His ministry (Matthew 3:13-17); (b) the coming of the Holy Spirit on the believers at Jerusalem before they were to go out in ministry (Acts 1:4-8 and 2:1-13); (c) the Samaritan believers receiving the Holy Spirit (Acts 8:14-17); (d) the Spirit-baptism of Gentiles (Acts 10:44-11:18); (e) the gift of the Holy Spirit to the disciples at Ephesus (Acts 18:24-19:7).

We carefully studied the arguments which said that the baptism of the Spirit was only a historical event that all modern Christians automatically cash in on when they believe. It was a complex debate, but we concluded that it was unconvincing in the light of the least complicated message of Scripture; it was certainly unconvincing given the bountiful fruits we observed among believers who were appropriating this special power of the Spirit. Our struggle was long and deliberate, but we finally decided that we would be the losers if we rejected something valid, even if somebody else had taken it to an excess. Certainly some of the Pentecostals we had known in the past were imbalanced, but that did not mean they did not have a grain of truth.

Finally I noticed that in I Corinthians 14, the

very chapter I had used to condemn many charismatics because they seemed to give it no heed, Paul specifically said that speaking in tongues is *not* to be forbidden (vs. 39). Paul was calling for balance; I had held an unbiblical extreme.

In honesty we admitted that we often lacked power to minister to others in a life-changing way. Hard situations slipped through our fingers, even though we wrestled to shape them into what they should be. We came to see that living by the power of the flesh didn't necessarily mean a life of evil; it was simply the struggle of a Christian to live righteously in his own strength. It can be done (more or less)—but oh, what effort! When we did the right thing in helping people we'd say that God had been with us and had guided us, but it was very seldom supernatural in nature.

So we prayed that God would grant us that same power that Christ had promised the first believers, and we asked that His Spirit would fill us and use us in a new way, making available those special gifts that are distinctly beyond human resources. As we recognized our weakness to really minister, it was a prayer of confession for having so long snubbed God's offer.

God answered our prayer, and a new experience with the reality of the Holy Spirit quietly but surely began.

Life in the Spirit is too new to us to share extensively what it can mean, and some good contemporary writing has been done by others. But there has been a major difference in our approach to faith and life as we are learning to act while believing that the Holy Spirit is working through us. I have experienced again and again the active choice I can make to "do it myself" or to open myself to what the Spirit wants to do. Neta expressed recently to the Reba Place community, "Something new and exciting is happening—a whole new freedom to truly give my life to God without holding back, without trying hard to 'make it happen,' trusting Him completely with my future, no matter what it is." One change has been major healing from our defensive posture toward the Christian faith to one of expectancy, praise, and joy for the reality and relevance of Christ in us and in others.

Admittedly, we've only begun. We sense a great deal that the Holy Spirit wants to teach us. But it's exciting to realize there is no limit on the available power to grow and to minister, and we are growing in the faith to exercise that power.

Looking back at the various communities we visited and those we've heard about since, we realize that the ones experiencing the most vitality were those opening themselves to the power of the Holy Spirit.

This baptism of power does not necessarily mean maturity. The Word of God, for instance, a large charismatic group of about six hundred in Ann Arbor, Michigan, was young and enthusiastic. Our visit was brief, but many areas of radical discipleship (characterized by Jesus' teaching on the Sermon on the Mount) seemed to us undeveloped. Their life together was just in its fledgling stages. But from reports we've heard since, maturity is coming in these areas of discipleship.

Commenting on the charismatic movement, Virgil Vogt at Reba Place said, "Like new life in

Christ, the baptism of the Holy Spirit is not meant to remain an individual experience, but achieves its fullness in the corporate life of a Body. What we need today are not just Spirit-filled individuals but groups of people who have the power of the Holy Spirit."

John Lehman, another Reba elder, explained this to us more fully. "Probably the worst cause of excess or misuse of the gifts of the Spirit has been the lack of corporate responsibility. The hit-and-run healing evangelist, for instance, has no one to whom he is responsible.

"Charismatic gifts in the context of the church-community, however, add the whole realm of accountability for use of the gifts."

This is true. Church of the Redeemer, for instance, was an *environment* where healing could take place. Miracles did occur, but it wasn't merely a "pray once, everything's OK" approach to the ministering gifts. Discernment, accountability, and daily support were all part of the ministry which grew out of their life together.

36

The Witness and Relevance to Society

(DAVE)

As Jesus rode on a donkey down the little road along the Mount of Olives, the disciples announced in loud voices to the people who were thronging along the way: "Blessed is the King who comes in the name of the Lord!" But when Jesus came to a point where He could see the city of Jerusalem, He wept, saying, "If you had known in this day, even you, the things which make for peace! But now they have been hidden from your eyes." Once in the city, "He entered the temple and began to cast out those who were selling" (Luke 19:38,42,45).

These few events began the last week before Christ was crucified, and they teach us our responsibility to society. First the disciples preached the good news, the gospel that the King has come, that God will forgive sin and free captives. This evangelistic role is the primary response God has commissioned the follower of Jesus to give the society around him.

Also noteworthy is Jesus' resistance to the improper response of the people. For nearly three years He had been teaching them about the Kingdom and what they must do to enter it. But in that moment the people could think only of political revolution. They wanted to use the methods of the world's system to accomplish the ends of the new order. They failed to see that such a compromise of methods would destroy the new order's character. Even if Jesus had succeeded in overthrowing Rome by such means, He would have set up nothing more than another phase of the old. Christ refused to pollute the new and make it old.

Also part of this tableau is Christ's cleansing of the Temple. Without purity at the core, there is no hope. Christ's actions were a prophetic challenge to the power centers and their corrupt practices. It seems clear that the small whip of a few cords that Jesus carried was not the real force that drove out the money changers. We understand what happened only if we see that they left in stunned humiliation at Jesus' condemnation of their unrighteousness.

The week ended with Jesus' arrest and crucifixion. This too represents the Christian's response to the evil of the world's system. We are to be willing to suffer at its hands. We are to expect to suffer, to follow Christ, and be sacrificed. We can absorb the evil results of this world's hate and self-interest because we know that we are following

Christ. "If when you do what is right and suffer for it you patiently endure it, this finds favor with God. For you have been called for this purpose, since Christ also suffered for you, leaving you an example for you to follow in His steps" (1 Peter 2:20,21).

These four things—spreading the good news, the distinct alternative to worldly means, a strong prophetic witness against evil, and the triumph of suffering—are to be the Christian's basic response to society.

This response to evil is different from anything the world attempts. It rejects the violence and coercion of the revolutionary stance that would do evil that "good" might come from it. And it is impatient with the gradualism of the reformer who would negotiate and compromise toward some hoped-for improvement. The Christian knows that the reformer's ideals will be corrupted more than the corruption will be reformed.

The church-community witnesses to God's better way. We may live in the new order now without violence and without compromise because of one solid belief: Jesus is really King. Nothing can ultimately happen without His consent. Satan and his forces are being permitted a time of freedom to work all the evil and chaos they can manage. But they will be brought to their knees in defeat. We Christians are called now to stand as a light, a city on a hill. Our tactics are to be pure, and we are to lay down our lives, not adopting the enemy's tactics and thereby denying Christ.

For years I had been uncomfortable with the teaching that the Christian should be concerned only with men's souls ("Change society by changing men's hearts"). I felt that this was true, yet it allowed too many churches to avoid a definite stand against injustice, or to speak on behalf of the oppressed and minister to the needs of the poor. On the other hand I had to admit that the Band-Aid efforts of many liberal churches failed to reach the heart of the problem; well-meaning efforts were often futile.

There is truth in the claim that Jesus is the answer. But that must be more than the declaration of a fly-by-night evangelist. The church-community offers Christ's whole message of healing from sin. We need evangelism, but we need something to call people into—a Body where they will be healed, supported, and instructed. Nothing is more important for the world to see than the real alternative at work. The gospel ceases to be rhetoric and becomes a way of life.

We should, of course, support the positive things that go on in this world's system, just as we should prophetically speak out against evil and even put ourselves sacrificially in its way. As members of the Kingdom we respond in Christ-like ways to what is good and what is evil when we encounter it. Different communities have felt called to different tasks in this response. We have already mentioned how Koinonia Farm challenged racism head-on and provided housing and jobs for many of the poor in their area. The People's Christian Coalition, a group in Chicago called into a common life as the Body of Christ, has a strong prophetic witness to existing political structures. The Bridge in Kansas had a special ministry for those in prison. Several urban communities have been placed by God in racially changing neighborhoods to give witness to how God's people can live in peace on a personal level. Peacemaking extends to the national level; most church-communities that we visited did not participate in war but worked for peace. Church of the Redeemer's ministering households were able to offer the emotionally disturbed, addicted, or otherwise broken person twenty-four-hour care unparalleled in quality by secular institutions. They were recognized as a major positive influence in their neighborhood.

We point to Jesus, and we are His Body here on earth. The responses mentioned above are some of the responses of the new order. But the most comprehensive message of His Body is to call people out of the old order and into the new. The best thing we can tell individuals in Washington or Moscow or any other bastion of earthly power is that they need to enter God's Kingdom. No list of reforms is long enough to change what they are about. Certainly there are degrees of evil, but whether Christ was speaking to the publicans and tax collectors or to the righteous Pharisees, He had one basic message: You must be born again; you must quit the old order and join the new. Actual Christian communities make that possible in more than theory.

37

Is This the Only Way?

(DAVE)

Usually the question, "Do you think this is the only way?" comes up early in any conversation about church-community life. Anything which details so many changes for the average person's life presents a difficult challenge. We have saved the question of whether this is the only way until the end so that it will be more clear just what "this way" amounts to.

If we were merely suggesting one of many options, it could easily be left open—adopt it or not, as you wish. But to a degree we believe that what we are saying *is* the only way. We're not saying that every Christian must live in an extended household, participate in a common purse, or adopt some of the other external forms we've described. But believers need to relate to each other in a fundamentally different way than most do at present.

The term *community* is only a convenient and descriptive word we've used to represent the practical expressions of qualities many Christians understand only in mystical or "spiritual" terms. It's not an empty word of theory; we've spoken of specifics and called for some kind of detailed action.

Most Christians ascribe to the godly life the qualities of sharing, sacrifice, responsibility, accountability, laying down self, and love. But few Christians see the necessity of altering their life patterns from the norms of the society around them in order to implement these qualities. They will share a cup of sugar when a neighbor runs out, sacrifice a couple of hours a week or as much as ten percent of their income to the church, accept responsibility for teaching a twenty-minute Sunday school lesson, etc. But any non-Christian will do similar things as a matter of personal interest or mutual exchange. Such shallowness proves nothing.

We believe that the only way we can please God is by acting in deed and truth rather than word and platitude. The Spirit may give various forms to this kind of action, but it must result in a more radical involvement than most of today's Christians experience.

To what end is this the only way? It is not the only way to get to heaven, nor are the only true Christians those practicing community. Many devout and genuine believers do not live in community (though God may force a change by allowing persecution in the future). And we are not saying that God can work only through community. He is not bound by our lack of understanding. He has worked mightily in all kinds of circumstances and through all kinds of people without putting His stamp of approval on everything they represent. And finally, we are not saying that we or any of the church-communities we've visited have the answers to everything. The Spirit wants to teach us much more in every area.

The external forms employed by the early churches, practiced by the communities we've visited, and described in this book are not the essence of the Church, but servants to the principle of the Body of Christ. We are not saying that they are the only way. If other forms serve the central principle of Christ's Body, fine. But if they merely produce an occasional sense of community, they are inadequate.

We are certain of one thing: our past life as "free-lance" Christians was not biblical. God expects each local church to be the unified Body of Christ in which the whole life of each member is coordinated in full-time, sacrificial service to Christ and to others. That, when practiced, makes a community. And although there may be a few variations, that degree of literal love and unity is the only way He wants His Church to be.

Epilogue:

Starting Anew

(NETA)

The end of this book celebrates a new beginning for us personally. The Holy Spirit used our visits to the various communities, the scriptural study that went into preparation for the book, and the process of writing to ask us again and again, "Are you listening? Are you prepared to do what I'm asking you to do?" A series of amazing events made it clear that the Lord was preparing us personally and Common Circle as a whole for a major change. Before the manuscript even went to the publisher, that direction solidified into a move. Dave, Julian, and I became part of the church-community at Reba Place Fellowship.

Working on a book of this nature has been a unique experience, primarily because we were so personally involved at each step. We were not only writing about community, but working it out in our lives each day. Time and time again work on the book had to take second place to needs that arose in our household. Or work would grind to a halt as we both struggled personally and as a group with some of the implications of what we were writing about.

Dave and I shared with Common Circle a growing conviction that God wanted us to be part of a full expression of His Body, the Church. And however much Common Circle meant to us, it was not in its present form the full expression of the Body of Christ that we needed. In response, our household decided to have a weekend retreat for the express purpose of discovering God's will for the future of our group. We had come to the point of realizing we had to finally answer a question Virgil Vogt had asked us a year before, "Do you consider yourself a church?"

During our concentrated weekend everyone agreed that the purpose for a group of Christians was to be "a church." But we also agreed that (1) we were at different levels of commitment to that purpose, and (2) we did not have the necessary gifts and resources within our group to be a church. We therefore had to decide whether Common Circle should join with another group or disband so individuals could go where the Lord led them.

It was a hard decision to make, because it carried the possibility that we might not be together in the near future. But each of us confirmed the decision as a positive step for our small community, one we were ready for. Paradoxically, the process of making that decision brought us closer together than we'd ever been before.

The next few months were a struggle as we sought the specific direction God had for us. But underneath it all we had confidence as a group that we had made the right decision. The Lord made it clear that Dave, Julian, and I should join with the brothers and sisters here at Reba Place Fellowship.

God has brought us back into community with Jan and Gary Havens (who currently have two preschoolers, a thirteen-year-old foster son, and a baby on the way). Their coming to Reba Place was totally God's doing, but it confirmed a sense we've had for years that what He had begun with our two families over three years ago He would complete. I have this confidence, too, about what God wants to do with our former "family" at Common Circle, even though we are no longer together as a group.

Our life here at Reba? Something exciting is happening—a new freedom to give our lives to God without holding back, without trying hard to make it happen, trusting Him completely with our future no matter what it is. "We know love by this, that He laid down His life for us; and we ought to lay down our lives for the brethren" (1 John 3:16).

We have described what is next for us. But an obvious question at the end of a book such as this is one a reader may ask: "If I believe that the Lord is leading me (or our group) in this direction, what next?" It would take another major piece of work on "Starting Christian Communities" to answer that question adequately. But here are a few ideas:

The most desirable direction to go in building Christian community is to renew established congregations. The greatest witness to us in this regard was Church of the Redeemer in Houston, Texas, an Episcopal congregation the Holy Spirit has renewed and channeled into community life and ministry.

A church ripe for this kind of renewal would probably show these four marks: an awareness of the desperate condition of the Church today with its lack of power and love; the hunger of individuals for fellowship and for effective ministry to needs about them; the conviction based on Scripture that God will act as He said; and a willingness to be open to the leading of the Holy Spirit without fear of change and no matter what the cost.

Renewal must come through the pastor and church leadership. A layman concerned about building community should, in a loving spirit, go to his pastor and share his needs and concerns. The proper place to start is study of the Scriptures over a period of time to help the church see that these things have the weight of biblical authority. Above all, forms of community should be implemented only when the whole church sees that they have a responsibility to "bear one another's burdens" in the name of Christ.

Many churches are not at this point. However, Christian communities can begin in a number of other ways: a large community may divide or a new group may spring up in a new place when Christians realize what life in the Body of Christ should be like.

If a new group forms, it needs to be more than a few good friends getting together to share a common life. Such a group would have value but at best is limited in what it can accomplish. Such a gathering should not be confused with a church-community, which must be willing and able to take on full responsibilities for building up the Body of Christ.

If you are just one or two, on the other hand, pray that the Holy Spirit will bring you together with other Christians who also wish to build Christian community. Share your thoughts with others, and begin praying with those who respond.

If a group of such people emerges, spend a good deal of time sharing. Don't get hung up on specifics such as, "How would we work out a common purse?" or "How would the work get done?" Rather, talk about commitment to the Lord Jesus Christ and to each other as brothers and sisters in Christ. Talk about what that commitment means for each person. Go forward on the basis of that commitment, and trust the Lord to work out specifics.

A group needs to be aware of its nature. Many Christian households or communities have formed around a specific project or task, and this kind of group can often accomplish something very particular in the name of Christ. But a group formed around a narrow-interest project cannot be called a church-community. *Being a church* demands a broad self-understanding. Such a group must be willing to bring into the Kingdom any person willing to give his whole life to Christ, and this should not be based on whether he can contribute to a particular project.

The Holy Spirit often directs a church-community to a particular task, perhaps even for an extended time, but that task is subject to the community, not the community to the task. In a narrow-interest group, if the task or project comes to an end, so will the group. But if a task or project comes to an end in a group with a broad understanding of itself, the community will still continue.

A church-community must have a core of mature believers with experience in Christian community. This is different from their amount of Christian experience. A group with no experience in Christian community should seek help from an older community. Many young or small Christian communities around the country have received significant guidance, for instance, from Reba Place Fellowship and Church of the Redeemer.

(In the New Testament, a group of Christians in a new place almost always received significant help from larger, experienced groups. These new groups usually began with the oversight from leaders from other groups who came to stay anywhere from six months to several years.)

Even a group which has experience in Christian community should have regular contact with other Christian communities so they can share certain responsibilities for each other, provide help in time of need, and question each other in areas of faith and practice. This mutual responsibility strengthens the local group and builds unity in the larger Body of Christ.

Many Christian communities began with just a handful of people. But a group that remains just a half-dozen will have difficulty functioning as a vital church-community. Size does make a difference in the stability of a group, its ability to minister, and even the strength of its corporate witness.

I am not saying that "success" is equated with numbers. Often the Lord may stabilize a community for a time of maturing, preparing it for future growth and ministry. But a group that is too small will lack gifts necessary for building up the Body of Christ. A group should be ready to grow if their life together is bearing fruit.

A community of God's people needs to determine the spiritual gifts among them. If it lacks such a crucial one as the gift of teaching Scripture, for instance, it cannot fulfill the responsibilities of being a church.

A group that lacks necessary gifts might (1) pray that the Holy Spirit will send the right people to join them; (2) seek whether the Lord wants them to join another group; (3) ask an older, experienced community to send mature individuals or families to give strength to the community until it has grown to the point where it can continue on its own.

An individual or family who feels alone in its desire for Christian community may want to seek out a community mentioned in the body of this book or in the appendix. Though these groups cannot satisfy the merely curious, they welcome persons sincerely seeking.

This has largely been our story—our search for the church in community and the fullness of life we have found. Much more is happening all across the country and around the world. Community is a gift the Holy Spirit is pouring out again on the Church today.

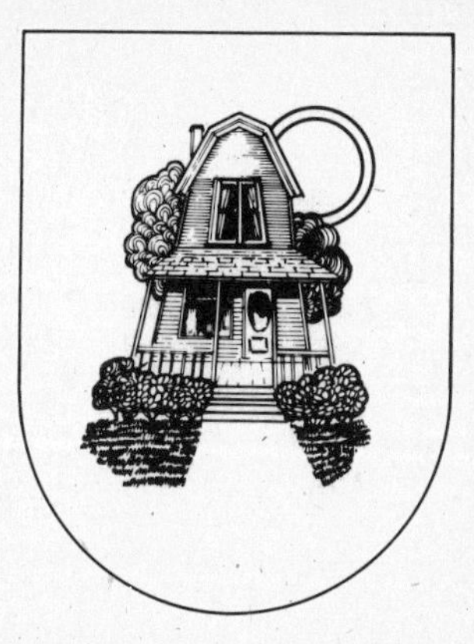

A Selected List of Christian Communities

The following list is a partial list of contacts for interested persons. The communities vary considerably in life-style and ministry and are at different places in their development. By listing them here we are not automatically endorsing all points of doctrine or practice. Although full church-community has been the thrust of this book, not all these communities have that self-understanding. However, we have personally visited over half of the communities listed below (those with the asterisk) and rejoice in the fellowship we shared as brothers and sisters in Christ. We are grateful for what we were able to learn in each place and for the love shown to us.

The Ark

70 Bellevue Ave., Springfield, Mass. 01108
Contact persons: John and Mary Gibbs
A one-household community of two couples, one baby, several single men. Central to their thinking is what it means to be the Body of Christ and minister fully to each other. Among their ministries is a "house church" which meets at The Ark, Young Life activities, many visitors. They are anxious for contacts and sharing with other Christian communities.

Bethany Fellowship

6820 Auto Club Rd., Minneapolis, Minn. 55438
This missionary-minded community grew out of a church congregation in 1945. Five families felt called to "renounce everything and seek first the Kingdom of God." In 1947 a missionary training and Bible institute was started; the initial enrollment of 12 students has grown to 140. The combined community family of staff and students now numbers around 290. The community and the school are supported by the staff and students working together in a common industry, building Bethany Trailers.

Church of the Messiah

231 E. Grand Blvd., Detroit, Mich.
Contact person: Jerry Barker
A church in the midst of charismatic renewal, living in community and forming households in order to minister more effectively to each

other and those sent to them. Probably similar in many ways to Church of the Redeemer (see below).

Church of the Redeemer*

4411 Dallas St., P.O. Box 18155, Houston, Tex. 77023
Contact person: Jeff Schiffmayer (pastor)
A church attended by about 1200 persons, about 500 of whom are living in community with approximately 50 ministering households. A dying church in 1965, Church of the Redeemer has experienced miraculous renewal through the power of the Holy Spirit, and today is a thriving and ministering Body. The experience of this church is affecting many other churches and communities.

Community Farm

Rt. 4, Bright, Ont., Canada
Contact person: Fred Kurucz
A well-developed farming community which has been going over 40 years. This community has also begun several small rural industries. At one point in their history, Community Farm was associated with the Hutterites. In recent years the present community has experienced a charismatic renewal and has a particular emphasis on the Christian's relationship to Israel. The present congregation numbers 75-100 persons, including children.

Fairview Mennonite House

1505 Fairview, Wichita, Kans. 67203
Contact person: Willard Ebersole

A one-household community made up of four families and one single person. This intentional community is a part of the voluntary service program of the General Conference Mennonite Church. However, unlike other voluntary service units, Fairview sees voluntary service and community as a life-style, not a two-year alternative.

Fellowship of Hope*

1611 Compton, Elkhart, Ind. 46514
Contact person: Keith Harder
A small but growing church-community of about 30 persons, both families and singles. This community started as a group of about nine persons in a local Mennonite seminary struggling to find meaning in their church participation; a common life together gradually led them to corporate responsibility as a church. Most members work outside the community, many in the social services.

First Baptist Church

Chula Vista, Calif.
Contact person: Ken Pagard (pastor)
A church renewed as a charismatic community with about a dozen ministering households at present and many other ministries. From what we have read, this church-community is very similar in spirit and form to Church of the Redeemer.

507 Atlanta Avenue*

507 Atlanta Ave., Atlanta, Ga. 30315

Contact persons: Bill Milliken, Neil Shorthouse
A lively one-household community of about seventeen persons. "507" began in the fall of 1971 around two families and several singles who were involved in Young Life. Emphasizes neighborhood involvement such as beginning an alternative school, volunteer work, etc.

Forest River Colony

Fordville, North Dakota 58231
Contact person: Joe Maendel
One of the many Hutterite communities in the United States and Canada. Forest River, unlike some of the other Hutterian communities, has been open lately to contacts and exchange with other Christian communities. There has been interchange of people between Forest River and some of the older communities such as Koinonia, Society of Brothers, and Reba Place Fellowship; also exchange of resources and food. The Hutterites have many traditions growing out of their 400-year-old history dating back to the Reformation. All Hutterite communities are farming colonies.

Friendship House

1520 N. 12th St., Boise, Idaho 83702
Contact person: Frank King
This two-year-old community was formed as a result of one of Koinonia Partners' discipleship schools. The five couples which make up the group are basically involved in neighborhood activities and service.

Jubilee Brotherhood

815 N. Royer, Colorado Springs, Colo. 80903
Contact person: Sam Johnson
This small group of Christians, though new, is active in the welfare neighborhood in which they live. Direction and interest lie in "volunteer work primarily toward the aged and disabled, a semi-subsistence farming and gardening economy, strategic social and political involvement."

Koinonia Partners*

Rt. 2, Americus, Ga. 31709
Contact person: Al Zook
A farming community begun in the 1940s by Southern Baptist theologian and farmer Clarence Jordan. This community has suffered much persecution because of its basic principles of brotherhood, nonviolence, and economic sharing. Koinonia Farm has since become Koinonia Partners, its major thrust being the Fund for Humanity, which is making possible low-cost housing, employment in rural-based industries, and farm land available on a use basis to Georgia's poor. The community has about 30 partners plus many volunteers who come to work and learn (the community population when we were there was about 70 persons).

Laetare Partners*

326 N. Avon, Rockford, Ill. 61103
Contact person: Vic Virni
A community of about 10 persons begun by

volunteers who had been at Koinonia, interested in developing in the same spirit of "a partnership with God and man" in an urban setting.

Lighthouse Christian Ranch

Rt. 1, Box 28, Loleta, Calif. 95551
Contact person: David Wilmarth
The Lighthouse Ranch is just one part of a broader ministry of Christian houses and other outreaches in such diverse places as Anchorage, Alaska, Coquille, Oregon, and elsewhere in California. They are mostly young people from the counterculture who have found Jesus and have been led to a life together proclaiming the Good News. Though there has been considerable turnover at the ranch, the leadership the Lord has raised up among them seems to have stability and direction.

The New Creation Fellowship (formerly The Bridge)*

409 West 11th St., Newton, Kans. 67114
Contact person: Dave Janzen
Three families joined together in early 1971 to "concentrate their resources for the work of peacemaking and care for their families at the same time." Changes: one family has left, others are joining; the group, though small, is finding new joy and freedom being and ministering as the Body of Christ.

People's Christian Coalition*

P.O. Box 132, Deerfield, Ill. 60015
Contact person: Jim Wallis

The coalition in the past has been a loosely defined but active group of about 60 persons, primarily involved in publishing *The Post-American,* a newspaper actively witnessing to the Christian's prophetic role in society and politics. This group is now broadening its concept and about 25 core people are forming a church-community in the Chicago area; outreaches like *The Post-American* will be just one of the mission project groups within the community.

Plow Creek Fellowship*

Rt. 2, Box 2, Tiskilwa, Ill. 61368
Contact person: Conrad Wetzel
A rural church-community of about 20 adults and 25 children. Plow Creek was begun as a sister community to Reba Place Fellowship, beginning with four families from Reba. Recently Plow Creek has been able to become a separate congregation, although there is much interaction and cooperation between the two communities. About half of the adults work at jobs in nearby towns (including mental health and children's agencies); the other adults are constructing houses and a common building and developing the farm. One of the ideas behind the rural community is to provide a retreat place for persons, families, or small groups from urban communities, summer work possibilities for teen-agers from other communities, etc.

Philadelphia Fellowship*

4929 Morris Street, Philadelphia, Pa. 19144
Contact person: Wes Mast
This small but growing group of about 15 adults (mostly families) has been brought together out of many varying backgrounds —Church of the Brethren, Catholic, Reformed, Mennonite, etc. Some of the members still relate as laymen or staff persons in their denominational church. The group has been building a strong commitment to each other, and most of the members have recently moved in close proximity to one another.

Reba Place Fellowship*

727 Reba Place, Evanston, Ill. 60202
Contact person: Virgil Vogt
A rapidly growing church-community of 160 persons just north of Chicago. Many changes have occurred in the past year or so—developing ministering households much on the order of Church of the Redeemer, an eldership structure, a renewal of the Spirit in terms of worship and ministry. The community, which is a very diverse group today, began in 1957 with several families of Mennonite background, reclaiming some of the old Anabaptist vision of the common life and spirit of the Church, with true responsibility and accountability for one another in all areas of life. The community is supported by the various jobs held by the members; many, however, are involved full-time in various ministries within the community.

St. Gregory's Abbey

Rt. 3, Box 330, Three Rivers, Mich. 49093
St. Gregory's Abbey is a Benedictine order, and the 20 men who make up the farming community lead a disciplined monastic life. St. Gregory's is unique in that it is a Protestant (Episcopal) order and is somewhat involved in the charismatic movement. The abbey serves as a retreat center for many individuals and groups.

Society of Brothers*

(1) Woodcrest
Rifton, New York 12471
(2) Evergreen
Norfolk, Conn. 06068
(3) New Meadow Run
Farmington, Pa. 15437

The Society of Brothers has three communities in the United States. All three are supported by making toys called Community Playthings. Each community averages about 275 persons, including children of all ages. Their purpose, in their words, is to "live out the Sermon on the Mount" in a full common life of serving one another. Serious visitors and those seeking community are welcome; sharing in their life and work together is indeed a joyful experience.

Suruban Partners

1215 Clarendon, Durham, N.C. 27705
Contact person: Sanchy Welton
One of the offshoots of Koinonia; a community

of about 20 persons (including one or two families). The activities of this group include the establishment of the Vietnamese Children's Fund, tutoring, a Third World gift shop.

The Word of God*

500 Packard St., Ann Arbor, Mich.
Contact person: Ralph Martin
A large interdenominational charismatic community (largely Catholic in origin) of about 600 persons. Major gatherings include a large open worship meeting; the community is divided into four subcommunities which also meet in closed meetings where "the Lord can build us into His people." Though people are scattered throughout the city and also attend various local churches, the community is building pastoral (ministering) households and developing a more solid structure of community life.

Further Reading:

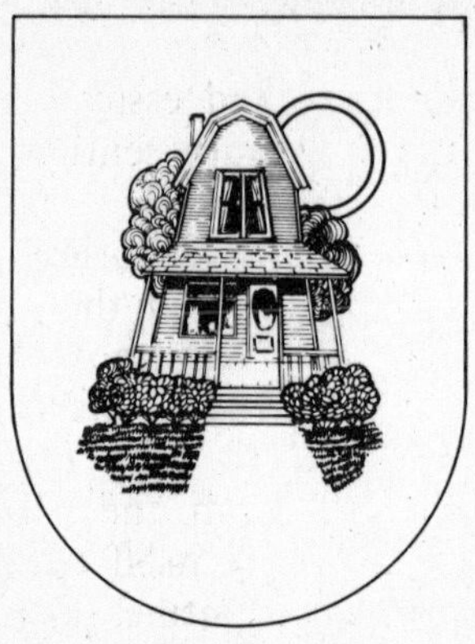

Annotated Bibliography

Arnold, Eberhard. *The Early Christians: After the Death of the Apostles.* Rifton, New York: The Plough Publishing House, 1970. $10.

An unusual collection of early Christian sources covering the period A.D. 70-180. Arnold, the editor and compiler, was the founder of the Society of Brothers in Sannerz, Germany, in the 1920s. Originally published in German in 1926, this book gives insight into the faith and practice, concerns, and life-style of the early Christians.

Its particular value for the Christian interested in community is that it shows that church life, as understood by the early Christians, was one of community.

Arnold, Eberhard. *History of the Baptizers Movement.* Rifton, New York: The Plough Publishing House, 1970. $.50.

A historical study and essay concerning the roots of the sixteenth-century Anabaptist Reformation. The study charts various church-communities even prior to the emergence of the baptizers from their underground status. The Waldensian movement, for instance, simply calling itself "Christian Brothers," is said to date from A.D. 315, when it split off from the official church, which had prostituted itself to the state and the emperor Constantine. The Hutterian communities, which began in the sixteenth century, are still with us today. When studied along with *The Early Christians* one can trace the repeated emergence of church-communities from the time of the Apostles until now. There are three notable peculiarities about these groups: they practiced community, insisted upon believer's baptism, and were pacifist.

Arnold, Eberhard. *Salt and Light: Talks and Writings on the Sermon on the Mount.* Rifton, New York: The Plough Publishing House. $5.05.

For the Christian interested in community life it recalls Christ's standards for living in the Kingdom.

Arnold, Emmy. *Torches Together*. Rifton, New York: The Plough Publishing House, 1964. $4.95.

In readable form, Emmy Arnold tells the story of the early years of the Society of Brothers in Sannerz, Germany—their life together, sharing all things in common. An important book in understanding the society's communities in the United States today.

Bonhoeffer, Dietrich. *Life Together*. New York: Harper, 1954.

Makes an essential point that community is a gift from God, not something we deserve or should try to create on our own. However, care must be taken not to confuse that gift with something hollow and mystical. Bonhoeffer was, after all, writing from the blessed environment of a literal community.

Clark, Stephen B. *Building Christian Communities: Strategy for Renewing the Church*. Notre Dame, Indiana: Ave Maria Press, 1972. $1.50.

Clark, a Catholic, writes from the perspective of renewing existing parish congregations. We found this a helpful book in forming definitions of just what is Christian church-community. It's valuable to anyone God has asked to renew a congregation from the top down. Clark is now with the Word of God, a charismatic community in Ann Arbor, Michigan.

Concern No. 14: A Pamphlet Series for Questions of Christian Renewal (February, 1967), available from 721 Walnut Avenue, Scottdale, Pa. 15683. $1.30.

This issue of *Concern* deals with the question of binding and loosing taught by Jesus in Matthew 18:15-20. As John Howard Yoder says in the preface, "It gives more authority to the church than does Rome, trusts more to the Holy Spirit than does pentecostalism, has more respect for the individual than humanism, makes moral standards more binding than puritanism, is more open to the given situation than the 'new morality.'" This zeros in on the nature and authority of the Body of Christ. It is an essential study for ordering a community's decision making, methods of discipline and understanding of itself.

Delespesse, Max. *The Church Community: Leaven and Life-Style.* Ottawa, Canada: The Catholic Centre of St. Paul University, 1968.

Similar in approach to *Building Christian Communities,* listed above. It was written by a Belgian Catholic priest who is one of the leaders of a movement for the renewal of church-community life in the Catholic church.

Harper, Michael. *A New Way of Living.* Plainfield, New Jersey: Logos International, 1973. $2.50.

This book is about Church of the Redeemer, an Episcopal church in Houston, Texas, which has become a vibrant Christian community of over four hundred people ministering effectively as Christ's Body. One of this church's major contributions has been its demonstration that the practice and experience of community is available to every Christian. The story of Redeemer is the dramatic transformation of a large traditional church into a loving Body of believers. We consider this book the most complementary to our own. Harper fills in areas we did not mention and speaks more gently to the successful and wealthy. But he is right on and very practical for the larger church.

Jordan, Clarence. *Sermon on the Mount.* Valley Forge: Judson Press, 1952. $1.95.

A down-home exposition of the Sermon on the Mount by Clarence Jordan, Southern Baptist theologian who began the Koinonia Farm in Georgia in the 1940 s. He applies Kingdom standards to modern life in a hard-hitting way.

Lee, Dallas, *The Cotton Patch Evidence.* New York: Harper and Row, 1971. $5.95.

Readable and engrossing story of Clarence Jordan and Koinonia Farm up until the late sixties. Takes the reader through the joys and struggles of forming community life, the hostilities and boycott of Southern neighbors, up to the new direction of the community now called Koinonia Partners.

Miller, John. *The Christian Way.* Scottdale, Pennsylvania: Herald Press, 1969. $1.50.

A study on the Sermon on the Mount by one of the early members of Reba Place Fellowship.

Pulkingham, Graham. *They Left Their Nets.* New York: Morehouse-Barlow Co., 1973. $2.50.

A book of "charisma, communalism, Christian witness" in Church of the Redeemer, Houston, of which Pulkingham is the rector. It is a fast reading story of the dramatic work of the Holy Spirit in renewing that parish.

A sequel to *Gathered for Power,* this book tells of the binding together of the first thirty or so persons which began the ministering community at Church of the Redeemer.

Reba Place Fellowship. "Reba Place Fellowship." Available from 727 Reba Place, Evanston, Illinois 60202. An extensive and descriptive brochure of life in the fellowship with clear explanations of the basis for that life. It includes many pictures. Free.

Society of Brothers. *Children in Community* (new edition). Rifton, New York: The Plough Publishing House, 1973. $5.95.

A delightful picture and essay book, both by and about the children in the Society of Brothers. Covers all ages. Includes articles by Eberhard Arnold on the education of children. Many more pictures than the first edition.

Stedman, Ray C. *Body Life: The Church Comes Alive*. Glendale, California: Regal Books, 1972. Paperback, $.95.

This book grew out of the "Body Life" services at Penninsula Bible Church in Palo Alto California, of which Stedman is pastor. Takes a big step toward understanding and practicing how Christians should relate to one another in the Body of Christ. However, there is a deficiency of Kingdom principles and their claims on the Christian and his life-style now. Another criticism by people who have tried to put its principles into practice is that it does not call for the practical commitments between people that can bring healing after they have shared their weaknesses.